MW00614130

-I Can-
FORGIVE
with God

OTHER BOOKS AND AUDIO BOOKS

BY GANEL-LYN CONDIE

I Can Do Hard Things with God

-I Can-
FORGIVE
with God

STORIES OF HEALING
FROM MORMON WOMEN

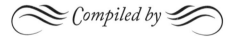 Compiled by

GANEL-LYN
CONDIE

Covenant Communications, Inc.

Cover image: *Cherry Blossoms in Japan* © ooyoo, courtesy istockphoto.com

Cover design copyright © 2016 by Covenant Communications, Inc.

Published by Covenant Communications, Inc.
American Fork, Utah

Copyright © 2016 by Ganel-Lyn Condie
All rights reserved. No part of this book may be reproduced in any format or in any medium without the written permission of the publisher, Covenant Communications, Inc., P.O. Box 416, American Fork, UT 84003. This work is not an official publication of The Church of Jesus Christ of Latter-day Saints. The views expressed within this work are the sole responsibility of the author and do not necessarily reflect the position of The Church of Jesus Christ of Latter-day Saints, Covenant Communications, Inc., or any other entity.

Printed in the United States of America
First Printing: August 2016

22 21 20 19 18 17 16   10 9 8 7 6 5 4 3 2 1

ISBN 978-1-52440-045-3

To Rob
Thank you for forgiving me today for what I
will do wrong tomorrow.

And to my children
Thank you for making me a mother. It is truly the greatest
honor and gift I have ever been given.

Acknowledgments

THE GIFT OF A LIFETIME came with the publication of *I Can Do Hard Things with God*. To bring its sequel to life has truly been a dream of dreams come true. I wouldn't be here without the support of so many wonderful people.

Thank you, Robert, for reminding me over and over again that there were more stories for me to tell. Your belief in me and in this work helps me believe the impossible is possible.

There would be no forgiveness book without the privilege of being a mother. Thank you, Cameron, for having the courage to share "our story" with the world. The past eighteen years have been the greatest ride of my life! I love you. Brooklyn, your forgiving heart blesses our family every day. Thank you for being patient with Mommy being at the computer—*again*. You truly are an angel.

Thank you to the amazing executives at Covenant, who took a chance on me and believed in bringing another *with God* book to life. What a privilege it is to work with such an extraordinary group of people. You are all so dedicated to bringing uplifting and inspiring content to the world. Samantha Millburn, you truly are the greatest editor on the planet. Your intelligence and steadiness makes the birthing process of writing not so scary. Kathy Gordon, only God knows what your example and influence have meant to me. Knowing you has changed everything. Thank you for leaving your thumbprint on these pages. To the loving staff at Covenant, thank you for making me always feel at home. I love being a part of this family!

Most importantly, I want to honor all the women who shared their courageous stories of healing. I cried as I edited your stories. I prayed as I read your raw words. I was inspired when I saw your faith. And I rejoice now as we, together, inspire readers to receive and give forgiveness *with God.*

Contents

Part V: Looking Past the Past

Foreword

by Mandy Davis Clegg, AMCHC

FORGIVENESS. BEING A COUNSELOR, I am frequently asked what it means to forgive. About how to forgive. We are not only asked to forgive, but we are also commanded to forgive. For clients, and myself, the process is both personal and profound. I, like everyone else, have had to find it within myself to forgive.

On my thirtieth birthday, at two in the morning, I was lying on my bedroom floor in the fetal position crying harder and, I'm sure, uglier than I ever had before. I had been on my floor since 10:00 p.m. With the way things looked, I was positive I would never get up again. In my mind, my life was over.

Just hours before, I'd found out that my husband had spent the better part of our seven-year marriage battling and feeding a life-threatening addiction. I'd discovered our bank accounts were empty and the home we'd nearly had paid off was mortgaged to its limit. I was told the banks would more than likely repossess both our cars, and I hadn't seen or heard from my husband in two days. Fearfully I wondered if he was okay. If he was dead.

Across the hall, our two beautiful daughters were sleeping. Little girls ages two and four. They were innocently and peacefully dreaming in pink as I lay there wide-eyed with terror, watching my worst nightmares come to life.

Lying there, paralyzed by my fear and pain, I said a prayer that would change my life. I said to God, "I think you are mean. I think you are a jerk! I cannot believe you are going to leave me here lying alone in the dark, not knowing how I am going to get up in the morning and care for those girls. Alone! On the anniversary of the week my dad, my fifty-seven-year-old dad, my perfect daddy, killed himself. I'm alone and still raw from not knowing why it had to be my dad. I'm here still asking why he did it and still believing I am partly the reason why. Alone! Not knowing where my husband is or if he is even still alive. And you, Heavenly Father, *you* aren't even going to let me feel my dad near me?"

That's all I wanted in that moment. I wanted my dad. I needed my daddy. He would have known what to do and would have fixed this! But he didn't come.

Instead, in the middle of that dark, cold February night, I learned the greatest lesson I have ever been taught. I learned how every single one of us has the ability to forgive and the blessings of receiving forgiveness. I learned that I didn't need another mortal person to make me complete.

In the darkness, I heard a voice—a calm, comforting voice—in my mind's eye say to me, "I am your Father, Mandy, and you will learn to rely on me."

And then I felt love fill my entire being. And I was changed forever.

* * *

Austrian psychiatrist, writer, and Holocaust survivor Viktor Frankl said, "When we are no longer able to change a situation, . . . we are challenged to change ourselves."[1] He believed that freedom comes when we have the ability to choose our attitude in any given situation. We are truly free when we can choose our own way without the entrapment of anger, resentment, and hurt. Forgiveness is a choice.

How do we forgive someone when they have robbed us of our peace?

---

1 Viktor E. Frankl. *Man's Search for Meaning* (Boston: Beacon Press, June 2006).

The first thing the Savior said after He was nailed to the cross was, "Forgive them; for they know not what they do."[2] I've read that sentence many times, and each time I do, I say to myself, "What? But they do know what they do! How can they not know what they're doing?" They just deliberately killed the Savior of the world. They just beat Him, stripped Him, mocked Him, spit on Him, forced a crown of thorns onto His head, and robbed Him of all His freedoms as they charged Him of a crime He did not commit. And they did all of this because they really didn't know what they were doing? They ruthlessly and barbarically nailed Him to a cross and raised Him up for everybody to see, for His friends and His angel mother, Mary, to see.

Hadn't Mary already been through enough in her short lifetime? *"Forgive them; for they know not what they do"*? But that is what the scripture says. And what the Savior taught and lived before He laid down His mortal life.

Then it all begins to make sense. He is the Savior of the world. He's barely mortal. He forgave them because He was perfect and knew where He was going when this whole nightmare was over. He also knew this was going to happen to Him. He knew it, and He had been preparing for it His entire life.

That's how He was able to forgive them.

But me? I'm just a human being. I'm flawed. I don't even compare to the Savior, so surely He doesn't really expect that of me.

But He does. And He sacrificed every moment of His mortal existence teaching us how we can live happily, peacefully, and free. God is the one person we can place all our trust in and depend fully upon to never fail us. He will help us forgive.

* * *

Each of us is going to have experiences that will require our forgiveness. Without forgiveness, we would become a slave to our hurt and pain. And there will be times when our imperfections and shortcomings will hurt someone else. I believe it is impossible to travel through this life without hurting another person, no matter how

---

2 Luke 23:34.

hard we try. This is our *humanness*. We are human beings, and by being mortal, we are meant to make mistakes. We will mess up—it is inevitable.

Having spent countless hours as a therapist, walking with and supporting people through their pain, I believe the only way we can heal, with God's help, is to turn our pain to wisdom. I have witnessed countless clients go from saying, "I will never forgive them for what they have done! *Never!* God would never ask me to forgive them" to "I knew I had to forgive them to find peace." Because of our mortal imperfections, we are here to learn, and each of us will find ourselves in situations where we'll need to forgive and in situations where we'll yearn to be forgiven.

I Can Forgive with God was compiled so that through the examples of other women, we can learn to forgive. Hope comes from reading the stories of other women and their journeys through forgiveness. Once again, Ganel-Lyn Condie has used her God-given talent to share true, heartfelt stories that not only teach but also inspire.

I Can Forgive covers many instances a person could experience in their lifetime that would require forgiveness. As you read of each writer's journey through their own suburb of Gethsemane, your heart will be opened and you will be strengthened. Thoughts will come to you about forgiveness that you haven't had before. As you feel the spirit of these women's hearts, you will be fed, lifted, and helped. These writers have candidly and selflessly shared raw experiences that will help you reach for and receive greater guidance toward forgiveness from a loving Heavenly Father.

Introduction

In October 2006, a thirty-two-year-old milkman lost his mind. Maybe it was triggered by the loss of his child. No matter the reason, he decided to enter an Amish school, tie up ten girls, and kill five before killing himself. He left five others severely wounded. As I began my work on this forgiveness book, this heart-wrenching story filled my mind and *never* left my heart. The profound mercy this Amish community expressed directly to the family of the shooter in the aftermath of tragedy stood out as the ultimate example of forgiveness. It stands as a bold example that forgiveness is possible. Even while wrestling with their own grief, many of the Amish attended the milkman's funeral and extended compassion to his family.[3] *But how?* I wondered. Could I be that forgiving in the face of such horror?

The example of the Amish elevated my own thinking. Can I do more as I consider how to be more forgiving within my own family and community? The reason I love compilation books is that each story teaches something invaluable. In this compilation, each woman shares a unique message and perspective. Their stories are both heartbreaking and hopeful: spouses working through the aftermath of infidelity; mothers, once little girls themselves,

3 See James E. Faust, "The Healing Power of Forgiveness," *Ensign*, May 2007.

now fighting to break the cycle of abuse and to heal. These essays range from everyday offenses to catastrophic losses, each one a personal account of God's love for His daughters as they walk, and sometimes crawl, along the path to healing.

God really can and *will* help His children overcome hurt, no matter how great or small the pain. The pathway to forgiveness may take time, but ultimately it can transform us. As C. S. Lewis once said, "To be a Christian means to forgive the inexcusable because God has forgiven the inexcusable in you."[4] God's mercy is there for each of us—the abuser and abused, the lost and the lonely, the hurt and the heartbroken. My prayer is that the reader will leave these pages knowing with absolute conviction that we truly can *forgive with God.*

---

4 C. S. Lewis, Goodreads, accessed April 27, 2016, https://www.goodreads.com/quotes/103229-to-be-a-christian-means-to-forgive-the-inexcusable-because.

~ *Part I* ~
MOMENT OF TRUTH

1
Tragic Death in the Public Eye
by Nikki Harding

I SAT IN MY HOSPITAL room alone, waiting for someone to make it for Tui's unexpected delivery. My water had broken a few days prior, and our goal was to stop labor with a hospital-appointed bed rest. I was thirty-two weeks to the day, and I was quickly realizing our little peanut was ready to make his debut.

It was April 9, 2012, just a few days shy of our youngest daughter's first birthday and our oldest son's sixth birthday. My husband was taking care of our four busy children while I was in the hospital. Chaos. My mom, our ward, and Kaj thought they had everything all taken care of and planned out. That was until the news came that Tui was not going to wait any longer. Kaj never would've made the delivery in time—so he sent my mom.

Tui was born quickly and was immediately whisked off through a window to the nurses waiting in the NICU. It was there that he struggled so desperately to cling to life. I spent every day for the next three months sleeping in a recliner next to Tui's hospital bassinet. I listened to uplifting music, read conference talks, studied my scriptures, and prayed fervently for Heavenly Father to give me the opportunity to mother this sweet baby boy.

My spiritual capabilities grew during those long, exhausting months. I had been wrestling with my testimony and personal convictions, but our family was working on being sealed, and this trial gave me time to study and learn. Little by little, I was growing in my knowledge of the gospel. It was a *long* process, but my life was finally on track. I came to know that The Church of Jesus Christ of Latter-day Saints was true and that I was a divine daughter of God.

The gospel helped me get past my fears as I watched our little baby fight for his life. I received a priesthood blessing, and my fears were quieted. I was told that Tui would live and that it was not his time yet. During those months, I consistently prayed and pled with my Father in Heaven to strengthen my understanding. It was real intent. I desperately wanted a spiritual confirmation of the things I was learning and feeling.

* * *

My faith was still immature, and my heart was seeking additional comfort. One particularly hard day, Tui was struggling to keep his heart rate and oxygen levels to the required minimums. I asked the front desk nurses at Primary Children's Hospital to please send out a page asking for a priesthood blessing for Tui.

That blessing ultimately changed my life.

At no point did they say Tui would live. It was not a blessing of healing like I was hoping for. However, it was a sweet blessing, one that gave me comfort and promised Tui the constant companionship of heavenly help. I had never felt the Spirit so strong and seen a change so immediate.

Tui made it through that day and many more. I knew then that I would never again question priesthood blessings or the power they had to heal and comfort. I made a promise in our hospital room that night to never lose sight of or forget the newly found truths that had been flooding into my soul over the last few months.

With the chaos of Tui's birth, Kaj and I made the rash and difficult decision that our family was finally complete. I'd struggled with each of my five pregnancies. Each of my children was born premature. I tried every kind of medication out there to stop my preterm labor and tried to prevent being placed on bed rest as early as twenty-three weeks. With so many young children at home, fear got the best of us, and we couldn't bear the doctor's warning that we might not be so lucky the next time. We were cautioned that it was only a matter of time before either I or one of our babies wouldn't make it through the delivery process.

I have always said it takes a special kind of strength to deal with the loss of a child. I was sure I didn't have that kind of strength. And so we decided our little family was finally complete. That decision was harder on me than I ever dreamed it would be, but I eventually found comfort and true fulfillment in my role as a mother and a wife. I sought the divine help I needed as I tried tirelessly to rear my busy children, all under the age of six, in the ways of the Lord. Our little family brought us complete happiness.

* * *

Months turned into years. I watched my children grow. I tried to pay close attention to the needs of each child while caring for Tui. Their little brother had slowly been taken off oxygen and was almost free of any signs of his preemie struggles. Tui was finally finding his place with his older siblings. I loved watching the older kids embrace him, including him in their games of hide-and-seek and house. His older siblings even taught him a few of their favorite knock-knock jokes. Our little Tui could make absolutely anyone smile!

Our children had become the best of friends, and there was nothing that brought me more happiness. We enjoyed morning snuggle fests watching *Daniel Tiger's Neighborhood*. We read books, made time for more snuggles, ate plenty of Otter Pops, and enjoyed long afternoons together. My kids' favorite pastime was singing lots of Primary and preschool-age songs. Every day felt like a playdate at the Harding home.

With so many blessings, my heart was full. I felt unworthy of such a blissful life, but I came to know that our loving Heavenly Father blesses us even when we don't always deserve it. I made sure to offer up daily prayers of gratitude for a life that far exceeded even my wildest dreams. I saw God's hand so abundantly in my life. Things were as close to perfect as they could possibly be.

The Call to Endure

"I have been driven many times upon my knees
by the overwhelming conviction that I had nowhere else to go.
My own wisdom and that of all about me seemed
insufficient for that day."

—Abraham Lincoln[5]

The day was so ordinary. It was one of those happy, laid-back, ordinary Saturdays.

There were *no* signs that this would be the day when our perfect world would change forever.

The kids had spent the morning Easter-egg hunting at their grandma's house. Now, in the afternoon hours, Kaj was outside helping our dear friends build a planter box for their growing garden, and the older children were outside with him.

I was inside preparing my conference notebook for the general women's session that would be starting soon, and Tui was supposed to be taking a nap.

When I heard him cry, I climbed the stairs and rescued him. He was a week and a half shy of his third birthday, but since he was our last baby, we hadn't moved him from the crib to a toddler bed yet.

I whisked him downstairs, made sure to wipe away his sweet little tears, and then raced the clock to put on the only pair of shoes that fit his chunky little feet. Of course it wouldn't last long—Tui hated shoes—but I made sure they were on when I handed him over to his daddy.

Tui loved his dad and was sure he was a real-life superhero. All of my kids wholeheartedly believed their dad was the *real, live Hulk*, which had created a special bond and sense of security in their relationship.

Tui knew he had cleverly gotten out of naptime and was excited to be free to play with the big kids. He leaped from my hands into his dad's strong, Hulk-like arms, and Kaj and the kids spent the

5 *Lincoln Observed: The Civil War Dispatches of Noah Brooks,* ed. Michael Burlingame (Baltimore: Johns Hopkins University Press, 1998), 210.

afternoon building, bike riding, and laughing with one another. Just the way Saturdays should be.

* * *

I gathered my things and committed to go to the stake center instead of staying home to watch the women's session like I usually did. My heart had been heavy with worry about our oldest son and the trials he was facing. I wanted to be sure I wasn't distracted and that I could receive the promptings and answers I sought, so I hurried out the door, binder and pen in hand.

I knew the kids were all outside playing. And since we live on a small cul-de-sac, I made the usual announcement that I was getting ready to leave and that everyone needed to be on the grass.

I located each child before I proceeded to back out, just as I always did.

After I had turned around, I noticed Kaj and a few of the boys walking home from the neighbors. I waited for them to get closer to the car, then proceeded to say good-bye.

Then, *once again*, I glanced around to see where my children were. I specifically noted Tui, who was holding on to the back of his daddy's legs as Kaj made his way to the house. Ryker was still coming home from the neighbors, but I made sure the other three children had gotten safely to the back of the cul-de-sac and were waiting for their dad.

That was the moment I started to drive down our street. And somehow it was also the exact moment Tui decided to let go of his daddy, perhaps to retrieve his wiggle car from across the street.

* * *

I never saw him!

When I felt the impact, I stopped immediately. I quickly looked around and realized my children and husband were still outside . . . and had just witnessed one of the most horrific scenes imaginable.

As I got out of my car, I saw what had happened. I knew immediately that Tui had been taken home to his Heavenly Father. And

I knew my little boy wasn't alone. But this tender mercy didn't stop me from begging that it not be true.

Clinging to a small fragment of hope, I offered a silent prayer, even while knowing he was already gone, that Tui would somehow survive. I clung to every bit of hope as I made my way to where he lay. I desperately looked into the eyes of the sweet mother and daughter who had stopped to help on their way to the women's session. Neither woman said a word, but I could tell by their watery eyes that my feelings were right.

It wasn't until I heard the first responder call off Life Flight that I was finally forced to let go of hope. Tui was with Heavenly Father. No one ever worked on him; no one administered CPR. The first responders let me lie with my sweet baby for as long as I wanted. They never brought out a sheet or told me it was time. Instead, they lovingly and kindly placed a baby blanket around our sweet boy. During that sacred time, my connection to heaven intensified to a level I hadn't known was possible while still in mortality.

Why Does a Loving Father Try His People?

The days following Tui's death were a chaotic blur.

My parents and sister were out of town for one of my dad's Iron Man races, but after being informed of the accident, they immediately loaded the car and headed home from California. Dad said he had never felt such an eerie silence as the one they felt driving home to Utah.

That night was the hardest night of my life. I felt so afraid, so alone, and *so guilty*.

My brain said it was an accident, but my heart kept asking, "What more could I have done?" This led to more questions. What had even happened? How had Tui been there at that exact moment? Why had I even decided to go to the stake center this year?

My world felt hopeless.

In that moment, life changed drastically. And I wasn't prepared. Our parental grief wasn't the only concern. Each one of our children struggled with their own tender emotions. As we carefully explained what had happened, their tears broke my heart. We kneeled together around our family room ottoman and offered up some of the most sincere prayers I have ever witnessed. Each child asked to say their own individual prayer. It was a sweet moment, one so sacred and so tender that there is no way our family would ever be able to deny the Spirit. Kaj and I knew we had been given strength beyond our own that day. Nevertheless, our children were heartbroken, and they were going to need us more than ever in the days and weeks to come.

The harsh reality of Tui's death meant that we somehow needed to find presence of mind amidst our grief as we selected a burial plot, made plans for the funeral, and dealt with the police, who were conducting a full investigation. Kaj and I had the heartbreaking responsibility of giving an official statement that Monday morning and were ushered back, one at a time, into the small, cold interrogation room just two days after the accident and two days before the viewing.

* * *

I was flooded with pain, anger, and guilt.

Denial came in crushing waves. Was this really happening? I wanted to crawl into a hole and wait for this nightmare to end. I spent the next few days in an intense, emotional personal battle.

I had made plenty of mistakes in my life, and they had all shown me what a life without the gospel would be like. I had even lived without the gospel for a time and knew the darkness and loneliness drifting away from my faith brought. I also knew that fully embracing the gospel and actively working on strengthening my testimony brought light and happiness. I'd felt relief in the past as I'd sought diligently to feel *fully* forgiven and to forgive myself for my mistakes. I had worked through the repentance process for years and had finally felt the healing power of the Atonement.

I cherished the feelings of forgiveness and love I'd experienced at the St. George Temple when, after five lengthy years, our family had finally been sealed for time and all eternity on December 1, 2012. Those feelings were the confirmation I had sought for so long. My heart had been changed, and I'd felt the easy yoke our Savior offers when we continually reach out to Him.

In those early days after the accident, I reflected on the promise I had made when Tui was born that I would cling to the truths that had been made known to me then. I held on to the testimony I had with every bit of strength in me. I knew I would need my Savior as I once again took a journey down the road of forgiveness. Thankfully, Heavenly Father had already prepared me and had walked this road with me before.

* * *

Constant flashbacks and the associated pain from the night of Tui's passing plagued me for months. Many nights they consumed me to the point of not being able to breathe. The anxiety would physically jolt me from whatever little sleep I had been able to manage. But over time and very slowly, I have turned to Heavenly Father and found relief and hope. Peace has miraculously been given where darkness so often threatened to overtake me.

As I started to work on confronting my guilt and forgiving myself *again*, I was able to once again feel the Spirit and begin to let go of the anger. My eyes were opened to be able to see just how present the Savior had been in our lives since the accident. We had too many angels to count—sent to help us through what can only be described as the depths of despair. Our Relief Society president and bishop were often our saving grace. They took care of the funeral, meals, and babysitting. They arranged plans for the cemetery dedication and for a celebration of Tui after the funeral. Having a party just for him felt *so right*. The whole neighborhood, three wards combined, came together to tie blue ribbons to trees, houses, mailboxes, and street signs throughout the neighborhood. What started out as being just the youth ended up including more than two hundred gathered outside our home on a Sunday night to sing hymns and Primary songs to our family. Friends, neighbors, and strangers all came together during our time of crisis, and the spirit they brought that night is something I still hold close to my heart. It was a sacred experience for me. It was the kindness and support for our family during our darkest hour that will forever be a testament to me that the Lord sends chariots of angels to minister both physically and spiritually. Tui's death led to my personal witness of the help we receive from both sides of the veil.

I often think of the scripture, "And he answered, Fear not: for they that be with us are more than they that be with them. And Elisha prayed, and said, Lord, I pray thee, open his eyes, that he may see. And the Lord opened the eyes of the young man; and he saw: and, behold, the mountain was full of horses and chariots of fire round about Elisha."[6]

In the weeks that followed, I found hope and purpose in reading my patriarchal blessing and following the counsel to "seek comfort in writing." Heavenly Father answered numerous prayers through writing and personal journaling. I had never been a gifted writer; in fact, I was never an exceptional student in any way, so to find comfort in writing and studying has been a huge blessing and necessity for my spiritual growth and eternal perspective.

However, feeling an abundance of the Spirit and witnessing a multitude of tender mercies didn't stop the question still lingering in my heart: *Why?* And because our story was a great tragedy, many different news stations covered it. We even had a few news crews parked outside of our cul-de-sac for days following the accident. What I initially felt was an intrusion by insensitive news crews ended up being a beautiful blessing in disguise. Every time our story was broadcast, I would immediately get a message on Facebook, Instagram, or on some other form of social media from someone who could relate to our heartache. Some messages were solely intended as expressions of compassion for our situation. Strangers and community members who reached out to our family will never know the lifeline they offered at that time. They will never know that their stories are what kept us from sinking, drowning in despair. They helped restore the hope and faith we had in the Savior's plan for our

---

6 2 Kings 6:16–17.

family, a hope we'd felt almost overwhelmingly before the accident. Through their courage of reaching out to our family, they helped me find some of the answers I was seeking to personal questions like "Why him?" and "Why through me?"

My Plan of Happiness

In time, some of the answers have been made ever so clear to me.

One is that this happened so we can help bring those who are seeking truth and forgiveness to a knowledge of their loving Heavenly Father and His perfect plan of happiness.

Tui's story has been used for good.

We have learned about families going back to church, neighbors letting go of grudges, and mothers hugging and kissing their children instead of being overwhelmed by the needs and demands of motherhood. We have even caught wind of a few people taking missionary lessons to learn more about our church. As Tui's parents, we find no greater blessing than hearing that his story has touched someone else's life for the better.

I know without any doubt that my family has been sealed for time and all eternity and that I will be able to not only see Tui again but also live with him in a state of everlasting happiness when this life is over. My children know they will one day see their brother again, and as a family, we cling to the promise of a sweet reunion.

Even then, at times, I still let myself wonder why.

I question why me, why him, and why us? But those thoughts are quickly overshadowed by the knowledge that Tui is doing the work the Lord needs him to do on the other side of the veil. He has an amazing spirit, and I am so blessed that we had almost three full years with him. He is working ever so hard, and as his mother, it is my job to continue that same hard work here on earth.

Process of Healing and Remembering

As a family, we have put hours and hours into creating and remembering happy memories of Tui. We have picnics at Tui's special spot.

We've done balloon message releases, picture books for the family, as well as for each individual child, and even a memory book of the funny things Tui would say. There have been quilts and teddy bears, paintings and drawings. Tui's crib was actually converted into a small bench our children can sit on during family scripture time. It makes our hearts smile when we see his little teeth marks on the railing. We have been blessed beyond words by the generosity of so many wonderful people giving irreplaceable gifts to us and our children.

But the gift our family holds closest to our hearts is from another grieving mother. She unselfishly gave our family permission to use her idea of creating a Facebook page in Tui's memory. Our grieving process has been made lighter by having something tangible to remember Tui by.

We launched Tui's Treasures shortly after his passing. We hide superhero toys whenever we need or want to remember Tui's smiley little face. We hide them while we are out on family vacations or trips to the park or for his month-mark "angelversary" days or at BYU games. And Grandpa hides them on business trips. We track these toys on our Facebook page. When someone finds a Tui Toy, they take a picture of their sweet little one's smile and then share it on our page. There are also options for others to print off their own tags and hide toys in Tui's honor. Now our family sits down almost every night to check his page and look at all the fun new places Tui's treasures have traveled. It brings our family such joy to see other children so happy. Tui was always smiling and brought such a special spirit to our family. Seeing his memory live on, creating so many smiles today, is another answer to why, because our family can't imagine living without it.

* * *

Three Lifelines

Grief and forgiveness are tricky, sticky things!

In many ways, I am still at the beginning of this bumpy road. But over the last six months, I have consistently journaled about three lifelines that have helped me cope and receive God's healing.

Bunker Down

Some days, I don't have it in me to seek for the answers to my whys or dig for hidden treasures in my trials. I have learned that it's okay to not push myself to new limits all the time. On these darker days, I simply try to weather the storm and not cave in to the overpowering waves of emotion. It's important to be aware of our fragile state and to be cautious of not pushing ourselves too hard. As the Lord reminds us, "Do not run faster or labor more than you have strength and means . . . but be diligent unto the end."[7]

Choose Joy

President Gordon B. Hinckley was the prophet when I started to develop my testimony. His words have always touched my heart in a special way. I find comfort in his simple teachings and sweet sense of humor. He said, "Go forward in life with a smile on your face and a twinkle in your eye but with great and strong purpose in your heart."[8]

I try to choose to be happy, to seek out the good, and to not be easily offended. I am grateful for the advice someone shared with me to not always listen to *what* people are saying but to *how* or with what *intent* they are saying it. I've found that most people are trying to offer help and love the best they know how. I have been blessed to be able to feel that love from almost every person I've encountered since our accident.

I try my very best to show love to my children. I want them to feel and see the blessings that have flooded in since the accident. One of my favorite things to do is talk with my sweet children about heaven. We wonder if Jesus makes Tui wear shoes, though Kynlie insists she sees Tui and that there are no shoes in heaven. The boys wonder if there are football games and ice cream in heaven. Whatever else it's like, we believe there will be a spirit of lightheartedness and unimaginable happiness. Imagining such a state always brings smiles to our faces.

---

7 D&C 10:4.
8 "How Can I Become the Woman of Whom I Dream?" *New Era*, November 2001.

When I am feeling strong, I choose joy—"Men are, that they might have joy."[9]

Cling to Hope

Life won't always be easy, and if we take the time to think about what the Savior Himself went through on our behalf, we should expect that there will surely be trying times during our mortal journey. But we can take comfort that there is always hope through the gift of the Atonement, as Elder Holland teaches: "If for a while the harder you try, the harder it gets, take heart. So it has been with the best people who ever lived."[10]

Sometimes all we can do is cling to our hope and faith in a loving Heavenly Father who knows these trials are for our *eternal* good. I know that Tui's passing was and is a special part of our family's mortal journey. Already I have seen many miraculous things come to pass as a result of the tragic events of that night. These things have enabled me to truly feel "that the Lord our God did visit us with *assurances* that He would deliver us. . . . he did speak peace to our souls, and did grant unto us great faith, and did cause that we should *hope* for our deliverance in him."[11]

I know without a doubt that our Savior knows each one of us by name. He knows the righteous desires of our hearts and loves us unconditionally.

While my mortal mind and heart still ache, my eternal self knows Heavenly Father has a plan for Tui and that his calling is being fulfilled on the other side—as he stands side by side with the Savior. How blessed I am to have been able to mother such a sweet and perfect little spirit.

* * *

Lately, I've been spending time in the mornings and evenings evaluating my grief and trying to figure out where I stand in my

---

9 2 Nephi 2:25.
10 "The Inconvenient Messiah," *Brigham Young University Speeches*, February 27, 1982.
11 Alma 58:11; emphasis added.

spiritual needs for the day. I seek help through prayer, scripture study, and priesthood blessings. I try to spend time in the temple when I am able—but at the end of the day, I pray that the Lord can use Tui's story to bring others to a knowledge of their Savior.

I pray that I will have the strength and courage to share my journey and the truths I have come to know. My prayers have been answered in knowing I am loved beyond measure. I chose to come to this earth and to bear trials that would test and strengthen my faith, for it is in the refiner's fire that the dark and unimportant dross is melted away, leaving behind a faith that is true and bright.

Heavenly Father has granted the desire of my heart to be home with my children as they find their way along their own personal journeys. I continue to strive to be the best wife, mother, and daughter of God I can be. I try to instill in each one of my beautiful children—Ryker, Briyler, Kajsen, and Kynlie—that they are divine sons and daughters of God and that they are loved beyond measure and have a divine purpose to fulfill. I hope and pray that my children will be able to learn in their youth how to endure faithfully, that they will be ready for whatever trials come during their mortal journey.

I have a testimony that our Savior, Jesus Christ, lives. I know that He loves us more than we know. He is a God of comfort and love, and He will never leave us alone. He is present both in our darkest hours and in our brightest days. He knows my heart and offers full forgiveness for my many mistakes and shortcomings. My Savior died for me and for that dreadful night when we lost Tui. Because of that selfless act, the gift of the Atonement, I can lay my burdens at His feet and take upon myself His yoke: "Come unto me, all ye that labour and are heavy laden, and I will give you rest. Take my yoke upon you, and learn of me; for I am meek and lowly in heart: and ye shall find rest unto your souls. For my yoke is easy, and my burden is light."[12]

It is this gift that helps us clearly see the wonder and beauty of life—even through the lens of tragedy. My journey of forgiveness and healing has expanded my view to an eternal perspective. My worth has been made clear.

---

12 Matthew 11:28–30.

2
Forgiveness at Church
Name Withheld

I DID NOT KNOW WHY.

Our ward Relief Society presidency had been asked to meet that evening with our recently called bishopric. My counselors, our secretary, and I had been serving together for only a short time. Previously, one of these sisters and I had served for a few brief months under another president. That president was a wonderful sister who had very faithfully guided the work of the Relief Society in our ward. But when her husband was called as the new bishop, she was subsequently released from her calling.

While we waited for a new presidency to be called, the other counselor and I were visiting with each other, and she asked me if I was worried about being called as the new president. I assured her that the Lord knew how chaotic my life was. Between full-time work, my master's degree program at BYU, and a myriad other life circumstances, I was confident I was *not* going to be called as the new president.

I was wrong, of course.

As in all things, the Lord knew me and my circumstances better than I did. He understood the ways in which I needed to stretch and grow. The Master Teacher knew the lessons I needed to learn. And so here in the classroom setting of the bishop's office, I was about to be taught.

* * *

As the door closed behind us, the bishop rose slightly in his chair, leaned forward, and looked directly at me. As he slammed his fist down on the desk in front of him, he thundered, "How dare you disclose confidential information about a sister in the ward!"

I was shocked. While I had no idea whom or what he was referencing, the first thought that came to my mind was, "*You think I actually did that? And so you've called me in here, in the presence of my counselors and yours, to publically reprimand me?*"

But in my stunned state, I said nothing.

He continued, and it became apparent that he was referring to a sister in our ward who had been disfellowshipped. He believed I had disclosed both her status and the reason behind her Church standing. While my mind whirled and I struggled to recall anything that would have led him to believe I had done such a thing, my first counselor spoke up. She declared that I had told them *nothing* and that the disfellowshipped sister *herself* had openly discussed these things with the members of the presidency and with other ward members.

I thought that perhaps with this misunderstanding resolved we could move forward with the purpose of the meeting. But the bishop *again* slammed his fist on the desk and asked about another confidential matter that had apparently become public. This time, however, I knew the source of the leak.

I glanced at the bishop's first counselor, who immediately looked down and away from me. Whether it was due to the incredible tension in the room or his recognition that his wife was the source, I do not know. But I did know that each of us in the presidency had either previously known or were realizing in that moment that this husband and wife were sharing certain confidential information. And this man's wife was disclosing it to others.

Not wanting to embarrass him in front of those in the room and not wishing to seem to be accusatory or defensive, I silently determined that this was not the time to address this particular problem, and I found sufficient voice to assure the bishop I had not disclosed that information.

With this second misunderstanding resolved, I again hoped we could move forward with the purpose of this meeting. But it soon became apparent that the accusations and reprimands were the purpose of the meeting. Next we were accused of thinking we ran the ward. This had evidently resulted from the way we were handling Relief Society callings. The previous bishopric had explicitly trained us to communicate with the other auxiliaries regarding callings and releases before submitting position requests. They also asked that we consistently and extensively track the status of callings so our very transient ward would not get backlogged on extending and filling them.

It was a large ward with extremely high mobility, and leadership had a goal to give callings to as many individuals as possible. Coordination with other auxiliaries regarding upcoming callings and releases was a means to this end, but when our new presidency was called, we met with the bishopric counselor who oversaw Relief Society to learn the *new* bishopric's preferences. Although we were instructed to proceed as trained by the previous bishop, these procedures and practices had apparently become a point of issue.

For the first time that evening, I voiced the question, "What would you have us do?"

It was a question I would repeat countless times over the next hours. The accusations and reprimands spun in circles around us, and it seemed that although we desired nothing more than to know what it was they would have us do so we could proceed according to their direction, we moved no nearer to any conclusive answers.

By this time, one of my counselors and my secretary were sobbing. My other counselor's astonished and confused stupor mirrored my own. We had been in this meeting and gone from home so long that one presidency member's husband called the bishop's office to check on his wife. Yet time continued to pass. We were emotionally exhausted. And the question "What would you have us do?" remained unanswered.

Eventually, the fuel behind the lecture was depleted.

Only one conclusion had come from the lengthy discussion— it was decided that we should no longer discuss callings and releases with other organizations.

We left the bishop's office hurt and confused and wondering why these misunderstandings and assumptions had been allowed to snowball into such a heated confrontation.

* * *

The bishop's wife later confided that when her husband returned home that evening, she had asked him, "Do I have any friends left?" This wonderful woman knew her husband's temperament and the toll it had taken on other relationships. Undoubtedly she understood many other things, some known and some unknown to us, which might have contributed to this good bishop's actions.

Surely the stresses upon the young, new bishop were great. Juggling the demands of a job, a busy family, and a large, highly mobile ward must have been incredible. Great must have been the pressures he felt and the weight he bore.

Whatever had contributed to the events of the evening, the question remaining for each of us was how to move forward. While in the bishop's office, I had asked him repeatedly, "What would you have us do?" Now I turned to the Lord and asked, "What would Thou have me do?" What lesson was I to learn? In what ways did I need to change? Where could I seek counsel and direction? Could I trust my priesthood leaders again? How was I to move forward?

I had many doubts, fears, and questions. But I also had trust in a perfect and loving Father in Heaven and in my covenants. There was never a question of changing direction, because I knew the gospel and Church were true; my only course was to press forward, even though I felt that each step on the path was somewhat precarious and that finding the next foothold would not necessarily be easy.

I sensed that my responses to the many facets of this experience could have a lasting and significant impact on my spiritual health. I wish I could say I handled everything with grace and without negative thoughts and emotions. But I didn't. I did, however, learn much over the following weeks and months.

* * *

Was I teachable?

I repeatedly asked myself this question. I needed to be prepared to learn the lessons the Lord would have me learn. As Elder Richard G. Scott would later instruct in a BYU devotional, I must be, as Alma taught, full of patience and long-suffering. "This is not an easy goal to achieve when you are wronged, unjustly criticized, misunderstood, or ignored. Yet when you sincerely practice this principle, you will qualify for the inspiration and guidance needed to resolve potential problems."[13]

In retrospect, what had happened was only a "potential" problem.

How I used my agency to respond to it would determine how real a problem it would become for me. The decision of whether to take offense or to forgive would decide my future course and determine the burden I would carry or the load I would allow the Lord to lift from me.

Elder David A. Bednar explained it this way:

> Certainly clumsy, embarrassing, unprincipled, and mean-spirited things do occur in our interactions with other people that would allow us to take offense. However, it ultimately is impossible for another person to offend you or to offend me. Indeed, believing that another person offended us in fundamentally false. To be offended is a choice we make; it is not a condition inflicted or imposed upon us by someone or something else. . . .
> One of the greatest indicators of our own spiritual maturity is revealed in how we respond to the weaknesses, the inexperience, and the potentially offensive actions of others. A thing, an event, or an expression may be offensive, but you and I can choose not to be offended—and to say with Pahoran, "it mattereth not."[14]

13 "To Establish a Secure Foundation for Life," BYU devotional, March 18, 2008.
14 "And Nothing Shall Offend Them," *Ensign*, November 2006.

Remembering always and holding fast to my testimony helped me immensely as I worked to forgive. I had been taught that while the gospel was perfect, the people who came to church each week were not. That included me, as I knew so painfully well. Only one perfect Being ever lived on the earth, and we, in striving to be like Him, all fall short of the mark. Elder Jeffrey R. Holland expressed it so beautifully: "Be kind regarding human frailty—your own as well as that of those who serve with you in a Church led by volunteer, mortal men and women. Except in the case of His only perfect Begotten Son, imperfect people are all God has ever had to work with. *That must be terribly frustrating to Him, but He deals with it.* So should we. And when you see imperfection, remember that the limitation is *not* in the divinity of the work."[15]

I began to study anything and everything I could find related to my experience. I wanted to understand the true principles of how we should work together while serving in the Church. I searched out general conference talks. I borrowed a copy of Elder M. Russell Ballard's *Counseling with Our Councils: Learning to Minister Together in the Church and in the Family* from a friend. I sought to understand the Lord's way of serving in unity. I don't know that I would have ever undertaken this course of study had I not had my experience in the bishop's office that evening, but I was beginning to realize that this emotional, uncomfortable experience was a blessing to me.

* * *

Each of the people seated around the room that evening has moved from that ward. In this laboratory of life, we were all brought together for a time to serve, learn, and grow. Given our human frailties, this can sometimes be a painful experience, but as Elder Neal A. Maxwell explained, "Unremembered by some is the reality that in the kingdom we are each other's clinical material; the Lord allows us to practice on each other, even in our imperfections. And each of us knows what it is like to be worked on by a 'student' rather than a senior surgeon. Each of us, however unintentionally, has also inflicted some pain."[16]

---

15 Jeffrey R. Holland, "Lord, I Believe," *Ensign*, May 2013; emphasis added.
16 Neal A. Maxwell, "A Brother Offended," *Ensign*, May 1982.

As a result of this experience, I have certainly been more reflec-
tive on the potential and unintended consequences of my words
and actions upon those with whom I serve. And though it's been
more than fifteen years since that experience in the bishop's office,
I clearly remember that in the following days, weeks, and months,
we each found ourselves addressing some strong emotions. There
were choices to be made. Would we follow the path of offense, allowing ourselves to fall away from the Church because we chose
to give greater heed to someone's words than to the witness of the
truth in our hearts? Would we relinquish the tremendous blessings
the Lord desired to give us? Would we turn our backs on treasured
friendships? Or would we hold fast to the truth and forgive, knowing Christ's Atonement was wrought for everyone's imperfections,
no matter the extent to which they might hurt us?

The husband of one presidency member was incredulous that
such a "meeting" had been held. In his disbelief, he went to the bishop
and valiantly expressed his thoughts about how priesthood bearers
should and definitely should *not* speak to Relief Society sisters. He
shared his concerns. The bishop expressed that it had not been his
intent to distress or offend and thanked the husband for his counsel.

Each of us had to work through our emotions and through the
process of understanding and forgiving, "lest Satan should get an
advantage of us."[17]

One presidency member made the decision that serving the
bishop would allow her to move forward. So one evening, she took
dinner to the church office, where the bishop had a long evening of
appointments scheduled. She later shared with me that this small
token of service was her way of saying to the bishop and the Lord,
"I am willing. I am open to healing instead of holding on to hurt."

I too desired to serve the bishop and his family. As I went to
their home, I was somewhat surprised when he warmly greeted me
with a hug. An awareness dawned on me—he had *not* perceived
that experience at all in the same manner we had. I felt I had been
given a glimpse, a vision of sorts, of the true desire of his heart,
which was the same as our own—we all desired to serve the Lord.

17 2 Corinthians 2:11.

It was a precious experience to recently attend, with another sister from that presidency, the wedding reception of the bishop's daughter. What a blessing it was to greet him and his wife, to embrace them, and to feel nothing but genuine love, friendship, and goodwill.

Time brings perspective.

I never expected to be falsely accused, berated, and publicly reprimanded, especially for things I had *not* done. But I'm grateful for it. I served with that bishop for only a brief time. He was released a few short months after being called, as his family moved to another city. I remained in my calling for some time after that, then was released and called as Young Women president.

Callings come and go. But what we take away from those callings stays with us always. I will forever be thankful that I had the opportunity to serve and grow with that good bishop.

This experience became, in some ways, a spiritual immunization. Just as some vaccinations have temporary and uncomfortable side effects, so did this experience. However, as I continue, even with all of my faults and weaknesses, to serve with men and women who also have their own human frailties, my immunization helps me to be strengthened against potential offenses in our service together . . . and I take greater care to ensure that I do my best to never be the cause of an issue for others. It is a blessing to me.

I learned that I can choose, no matter the circumstances, to not take offense. I learned that I will never permit an individual's actions, even those of a leader, to prevent me from standing firm in my covenants.

And I learned and continue to learn that I can and *must* forgive.

Part II
MARRIAGE

3

The Choice to Forgive: After Betrayal and Divorce

Name Withheld

I'M STILL NOT SURE HOW it happened. It seemed like one minute I was on the steps of the Salt Lake Temple, hand in hand with my eternal sweetheart, beaming for the camera and fashioning all the dreams that would carry us through our life together, and the next I was sitting in the lobby of my divorce attorney's office, dabbing blankly at tears that wouldn't stop.

But there was, in actuality, more than a minute in between— there were twenty-six years' worth of them, to be exact. Many were breathtakingly wonderful, including the experiences that surrounded the adoption of our children. Most of them were blissfully ordinary, and I thought they would last forever. But some of them were gut-wrenchingly difficult, like the suicide of our seventeen-year-old son and the revelation that my husband was using drugs.

Just two weeks after my fiftieth birthday, my husband—that once-bright-eyed young man who had clasped my hand so tightly on the steps of the Salt Lake Temple—walked away from our marriage. The day was bright, and sunshine warmed the rich soil of the flowerbeds along the front of our house. Crocuses had pushed tenaciously through the surface, followed by early tulips and the hint of hyacinths. We had spent a leisurely morning making plans for the rest of the weekend. We had discussed the dinner menu for Sunday—I wanted it to be special because it was my mother's wedding anniversary. More than forty years after my father's death, it was still a tender date for her.

Later that day, I prepared to run some errands. As I turned the key in the ignition, my husband moved quickly around the front of the car and scrambled into the passenger's seat. "We need to talk," he said. I still can't remember exactly what words he used or how he strung them together, but I do remember he told me he was leaving. That day.

He told me he could no longer stay in a marriage in which his spiritual ideas were not respected. I was floored. I'd had no idea his spiritual ideas were different from mine. His included permanently removing his garments, having strange visions that contradicted Church doctrine, and participating in "healing circles" to heal Heavenly Father's DNA.

More than a decade later, the rest of what he said is still a blur.

He got out of the car, climbed into his truck, and pulled away from our house. And then, so suddenly it shocked me, I died inside.

I managed to get back into the house and crawl into bed, though the hour was still early. It seemed to be the only thing that made sense. I lay trembling, staring across the expanse of the king-sized mattress. Suddenly it seemed massive. I prayed, pulling the quilts up around my chin and drawing my knees to my chest. I wept bitterly, tears of agony soaking my pillow.

I called out to my son who had committed suicide just a year earlier. Waves of anxiety, then fear, then utter betrayal washed over me and threatened to drown me. Between sobs, I frantically gasped for air.

After hours of anguish, I glanced at the clock. It was not yet even close to midnight. I feared I would not survive until morning.

Then it started again—the tormented weeping, the uncertain grief. I must have made more noise than I'd imagined because at one point, my sixteen-year-old son crept through the darkness and climbed cautiously into bed beside me. He gathered me up in his strong arms and took a deep breath.

"Don't cry, Mom," he said, feeling for perhaps the first time *his* chance to be *my* comforter. "Dad may have left, but you are not alone. You are worthy. You still have your sacred covenants. You have Heavenly Father, and He loves you. Dad leaving will never change that."

It was the first of many words of humble advice and comfort I would receive during the months ahead. Many of them, like my son's, came from sources I would never have expected.

A Meticulous Plan

The next morning, as word of my husband's leaving spread up and down the street like ripples from a stone breaking the surface of a pond, the facts began trickling in. I heard witnesses to his infidelity. I heard accounts of his iniquity. I learned of bold-faced lies and examples of unfettered betrayal. Perhaps most disturbing, I found out that he had planned this for years. He had established a step-by-step checklist of how to prepare for his life without us, and he had carefully and surreptitiously checked off each item. The day he left—a little earlier than he had actually planned— he'd had only a few loose ends to tie up.

For him, his exit seemed smooth and uncomplicated.

For me, it was incredibly coarse and terribly convoluted.

For him, it seemed casual. He had thought about it and turned it over in his mind every day for at least five years. He was used to the idea; it was almost second nature.

For me, it was brand-new.

I was baffled. Why hadn't anyone told me?

I remember sitting on the couch in my living room across from my mother, trying to make sense of it all. It was her anniversary— the day I had wanted to make so special for her.

Instead, I could barely function. I think I looked fairly normal on the surface, but I remember trembling inside so violently that it was difficult to speak. My heart raced. My stomach churned. My mind jumped from one place to another in no rational order.

I remember wandering downstairs to listen to conference and my heart breaking as I heard Elder F. Burton Howard describe his wife's tender care of their silverware—pieces saved for and purchased one at a time through the early, financially sparse years of their marriage. I remember him describing how she guarded and protected that silverware—even putting it in a safe-deposit box while they served a mission.

"For years I thought she was just a little bit eccentric," he said, "and then one day I realized that she had known for a long time something that I was just beginning to understand. *If you want something to last forever, you treat it differently.* You shield it and protect it. You never abuse it. You don't expose it to the elements. You don't make it common or ordinary. If it ever becomes tarnished, you lovingly polish it until it gleams like new. It becomes special because you have made it so, and it grows more beautiful and precious as time goes by."[18] It should be that way, he said, with our eternal marriages.

Eternal marriage. I used to have one of those. But I didn't anymore.

His remarks came at the end of the Sunday afternoon session. I sat curled up in the recliner in the family room, sobbing. I didn't care who heard; I was desperate to try anything that might relieve the pain. My mother, whose day it should have been, mobilized my children and scurried around the kitchen, fixing dinner for *me*.

One Day at a Time

Somehow I got through that day. And the next. And the one after that. And all the ones since then.

I won't lie: some were much worse than others. A few were glorious. Most were somewhere in between. I simply learned that I had to get through them one at a time. There was no secret pill, no magic bullet. There was no other way to get through; I had to do it just one agonizing day at a time.

Little by little, the pain that had so tenaciously attached itself to my love for my ex-husband diminished, as did the love itself. I learned with stunning reality that it's not easy to suddenly stop loving someone. Not nearly as easy or as rapid as falling in love

---

18 "Eternal Marriage," *Ensign*, May 2003.

is. I learned that falling in love is as easy as falling off a log and that falling out of love is more akin to being dragged through a vast field of ferociously thorny brush. But I did eventually reach the other end of that field. And by the time I reached it, I was not nearly as wounded as I had expected to be.

Friends who have never divorced—some of whom have not yet married—have asked me how it feels.

I guess there are as many answers to that as there are divorces.

A Sea of Aloneness

For me, it felt as though I had lost my anchor. I was adrift on an often turbulent sea. The water was so cold it chilled my bones. The waves were unpredictable and not infrequently frightening. The random creatures that brushed up against me in the murky waters were often menacing.

I was exhausted from frenetically paddling my arms and legs in an effort to stay afloat in an area where I could feel even a little bit safe. I could have relaxed—could have assumed the limp position of the dead man's float—but then the tides could have pulled me into places where I faced dangers I could not handle. No, I had to keep paddling. No matter how exhausted I was.

I yearned to find another anchor—a great, solid anchor that would tether me to safety and provide me stability. I knew I had a heavenly anchor. And as precious as that knowledge was to me, sometimes it just wasn't enough. Sometimes I felt I needed more. Something tangible.

Most difficult was that I felt all alone in that vast sea. As far as my eye could see, there was not another soul. For the first time in my life, I felt profoundly alone. I felt small—almost indistinguishable among the swells of endless rolling water—and frightened.

If I concentrated, if I focused with all my might, I could sometimes make out the blurred outline of the distant horizon, though it seemed shrouded in a heavy fog, still far out of my reach. Far out of any remotely possible grasp. Even so, I tried desperately to always stay where I could see it, tried never to get pulled so far out or with such intensity that I lost sight of it, because I knew it was where I wanted to be. And somehow I knew that, against all odds, I would eventually be able to get there again.

Pretending Normalcy

Initially, during those first weeks and months, that sense of being alone was the most difficult part of my divorce. In the first surreal days after my husband left, I desperately tried to avoid being alone. When there were other people around me—colleagues bantering in the hallway at work, kids arguing over who got to choose what to watch on television, my son-in-law drifting through the kitchen to microwave a bag of popcorn, friends wandering over to see what I was dredging out of the garden—I didn't have to think about what had happened.

I could pretend, if only to myself, that things were normal.

But in those quiet, cavernous moments of aloneness, stark reality always set in. Things were *not* okay. They were *not* normal (though I have since come to challenge that there is such a thing as "normal" at all). And they were definitely *not* as they had always been.

During those times, when I was forced to see my situation for what it was, I somehow found it less threatening to focus on the nuts-and-bolts, temporal side of things. I had no lawn mower; who would mow my grass? My husband had left the weed trimmer, but I didn't have a clue how it worked. Was the sturdy orange line *supposed* to be unraveling? What about my swamp cooler? I had never succeeded in climbing higher than the second step of a ladder, let alone onto the roof. Besides, I didn't know what to do when I got up there. Even more, there was no longer a ladder.

My daughter accidentally pulled off the front of the silverware drawer; now the drawer was jammed. What could I do about that? The refrigerator's filter light was on—there was a filter in there? What happened when the garage door opener stopped working? What if the hornets burrowed in under the front steps again and built another nest? How on earth could a shrub die so quickly? And why was the dryer making that horrible noise?

When I felt threatened by actual events or by nothing more than the underpinnings of my own imagination, I no longer had someone to protect me and keep me safe. Instead, I had to dig deep within myself for the courage to look bigger and more menacing than I actually was, kind of like the posture the park rangers told us to use when confronted by a bear.

As the days and months continued on, all of these things were overwhelming—but not nearly as overwhelming as the spiritual things, especially the things I couldn't bear to contemplate at the time.

It turned out there were far worse things than jammed kitchen drawers and dryers that went bump in the night. When something difficult happened with one of the kids—like the morning I found my twenty-year-old son dead on the family room couch, the victim of an accidental drug overdose—I no longer had someone who could square up his shoulders and help take the pain away.

Of You It Is Required to Forgive All Men

On top of all the painful feelings associated with my divorce, there it was in black and white: "I, the Lord, will forgive whom I will forgive, but of you it is required to forgive all men."[19] *All* men. Not just the nice, likable ones. Even the ones who weren't at all sorry for what they had done. And it was *required*. Not just an option.

I knew I had to forgive my ex-husband. After all, I myself desperately needed forgiveness on a constant basis. Each Sunday I approached the sacrament table with a prayer in my heart to be forgiven for the mistakes I had made throughout the week. I earnestly wanted to use the Atonement so I could someday return to my Father clean and pure. If I wanted that to happen, the Savior made my responsibility clear: "If ye forgive men their trespasses your heavenly Father will also forgive you; But if ye forgive not men their trespasses neither will your Father forgive your trespasses."[20]

It was a paralyzing thought.

---

19 D&C 64:10.
20 3 Nephi 13:14–15.

Can what the Lord says here really be true? Can failing to forgive be a greater sin than whatever sin or offense was committed against us? How is such a thing possible? Perhaps part of the reason is that our choice not to forgive *always* stops our spiritual progress, regardless of how grievous the offense against us might have been. By holding on to a grudge or by continuing to harbor hurt feelings, we prevent the Savior's healing balm from quickening the process of soul repair that He is always ready and able to offer both the offended and the offender. Our unwillingness to forgive and to let go of wounded feelings stops or damns our progress. We become stuck in an ever-tightening circle of self-pity, self-deception, and anger. We're trapped in a ditch we've dug for ourselves. Only in reaching for the Savior's outstretched hand can we hope for rescue.[21]

In those first few months—years, even—forgiving my ex-husband seemed impossible. There was just *so much* to forgive. Much of it was pretty big. He announced the day after he left that he was gay, and I learned there had been multiple affairs with men and women. He had contracted HIV and had knowingly and callously exposed me to that fatal disease.

He had abused alcohol and illicit drugs. He had ridiculed me behind my back because he'd casually left his stash next to the bathroom sink, telling me I was so "stupid and naive" I didn't even know what it was.

He had horrifically abused our children. He had destroyed the testimony and faith of my youngest daughter. He had sold drugs to and done drugs with my oldest son, the one who had subsequently died of the accidental drug overdose.

In our twenty-six years of marriage, he had worked only sporadically. During all twenty-six years, I had worked full-time and done additional contract work. By tricking me into a nonexistent investment scheme, he had stolen my 401k on his way out the door—as well as $11,000 in cash.

He had become deeply entrenched with a group of apostates and was deliberately leading others away.

---

21 Scott Livingston, *Beauty for Ashes* (American Fork, Utah: Covenant Communications, Inc., 2015), 68; emphasis added.

I was hurting. My children were hurting. I was financially, emotionally, and spiritually exhausted. How on earth was I supposed to forgive such a litany of offenses?

It was clear. I was supposed to forgive the same way my Heavenly Father does.

I never believed it was possible, but it happened. It took a long time, but it eventually happened.

I'm not sure I recognized it right away. But I remember the day it came with clarity like it was yesterday. I was standing in my kitchen, and as had often happened, I started to cry. But this time was different: I was crying *for* him, not *because of* him. I was crying for all the things he had lost—his marriage, his family, his testimony, his relationship with the Savior, his righteous friends, his covenants, his standing in the Church, his ability to walk through the doors of the temple, his discernment, the companionship of the Holy Ghost . . . there were too many losses to name. I felt great sorrow—not because of what he had done to *me* but because of what he had done to *himself*.

As that realization slowly washed over me, I understood that I was experiencing in the most minuscule measure what the Savior and the Father must feel as we stumble and fall.

I had at last forgiven my ex-husband.

And I had learned some valuable lessons along the way.

Forgiveness Is a Process

Before this, I thought forgiveness was an automatic, immediate thing that happened all at once.

It's not.

It's a complicated process that can take a very long time.

There are also hiccups along the way simply because we're human and also because offenses can continue even after we've removed ourselves from the situation. Just as I thought I was finally ready to forgive my ex-husband, he gave my youngest daughter marijuana to sell at school so she could have some spending money. When I found out, my journey to forgiveness took a big detour—my anger sent me directly to the jail square without passing "Go" and without receiving $200. I was frustrated with how long it took me to regain some equilibrium.

Forgiveness also takes time because it's not the only thing on the agenda at any given moment. We still have to live our lives, fulfill our responsibilities at home, serve in our Church callings, attend to our careers, show up for the school play or football game . . . and somehow fit the very big job of forgiving into an already exhausting and demanding schedule. I found that it happened for me a small bit at a time during those moments when I was kneeling in prayer or experiencing solitude or quietly cuddling with a grandchild.

Forgiveness is also a process because sometimes you have to do it over and over. Because my ex-husband and I share children, he will never be completely out of my life. Over the intervening years, I have had to forgive again as subsequent offenses have occurred. I have found it gets a little easier each time.

One thing that helped that process was trying to see my ex-husband as the Lord saw him. I am flawed, and my view of situations is subsequently flawed. One day I stopped to think about the fact that my husband had been sexually abused by a member of his bishopric for six years in his adolescence. And in that moment came a burst of understanding. Perhaps it didn't excuse anything, but it did help me judge my ex-husband less harshly.

It's Not about Forgetting

I always thought forgiving meant forgetting.

It doesn't.

Truly forgiving someone of an offense means dropping all the emotional baggage attached to the person and the offense. It means you can think about what happened without experiencing a sudden jolt of anger, hostility, hatred, or grief. Your heart doesn't skip a beat, and your stomach doesn't leap into your throat. You don't feel as if you are about to plunge over a precipice.

When we have truly forgiven, we may not forget, but our thoughts are no longer peppered with details of the offense. Yes, we may think about it occasionally—but with the passage of time, those sparks of memory become less and less frequent.

There are actually good reasons for not forgetting. Remembering helps us avoid falling into a similarly hurtful situation again; we remember what happened before, and we're more apt to recognize the red flags and spiritual promptings that keep us safe. Recognizing the traits my ex-husband had, even at the beginning of our marriage, helped me make a much better choice when I remarried.

Remembering also enables us to be of help to others who may find themselves in a similar situation. I have had countless opportunities over the last decade to counsel with, listen to, or simply empathize lovingly with others who have been hurting.

You're Not Responsible for Anyone Else

As I said, even after my ex-husband left on that balmy spring day, he continued to commit offenses. And though some of them directly affected me, most of them did not. He married his male companion in a legal ceremony. They became Wiccan and began practicing witchcraft. His drug use became so serious that it affected his cognition and ability to think and reason.

Before I managed to forgive him, every one of those offenses felt like a knife being plunged into my heart. But now I see them for what they are: His decisions. His behavior. His choices, complete with his consequences. I can feel bad about them and even sorry for them, but I never, ever have to feel bad *because* of them.

And just as his choices were not my responsibility, neither was it my job to worry about whether the Lord would forgive him. That was the Lord's decision, and He is infinitely more qualified to make that kind of decision than any of us. That was simply something on which I didn't need to spend my time, energy, or thoughts. And that realization brought a feeling of blessed freedom.

Forgiveness Brings Incredible Gifts

I likened my experience in the first months after my marriage ended to being adrift in a cold, lonely sea. That sea was my enemy. I was doing my best to keep my sights aligned on the distant shore, where I knew I wanted to be.

Once I was truly able to forgive, everything changed.

Most of all, I changed.

In her endearing *Gift from the Sea*, Anne Morrow Lindbergh reflects on her experience of vacationing at a quiet beach, settling peacefully against the cool sand, and watching the waves gently lap against the shore. This is how I feel my change happened:

> One never knows what chance treasures these easy unconscious rollers may toss up, on the smooth white sand of the conscious mind; what perfectly rounded stone, what rare shell from the ocean floor. Perhaps a channelled whelk, a moon shell, or even an argonaut.
>
> But it must not be sought for or—heaven forbid!—dug for. No, no dredging of the sea bottom here. That would defeat one's purpose. The sea does not reward those who are too anxious, too greedy, or too impatient. To dig for treasures shows not only impatience and greed, but lack of faith. Patience, patience, patience, is what the sea teaches. Patience and faith. One should lie empty, open, choiceless as a beach—waiting for a gift from the sea.[22]

Patience and faith. They are the qualities that finally help us achieve forgiveness, and they are the qualities I finally developed through the slow, exacting process of forgiveness. They are the qualities that kept me afloat, the qualities that made me understand that though I was still at times in the sea, I was not adrift.

Instead, I was waiting for—and discovering—the gifts of the process through which I was working.

I now recognize the sea for its calm. My heart is soothed as I watch the waves, even though some of them dash against the rocks with a force that inspires my awe. Its vastness now represents a sanctuary—a refuge where I at last found peace.

22 New York: Random House, 1955, 10–11.

Those are some of the gifts of forgiveness. Perhaps best of all is the sublime gift of *being* forgiven and of being able to forgive myself.

Not long after I had finally forgiven my ex-husband, I came across—for perhaps the hundredth time—the scripture warning us that at the judgment bar, we will have a "bright recollection of all our guilt."[23] At that time, as never before, I became filled with dread. I thought I had repented sufficiently—but what if I hadn't? Would I be standing there at the bar, horrified over sins that still stained me scarlet?

After beating myself up over that possibility for weeks, I finally went to the temple in an attitude of fasting and prayer. I did some initiatory work, then participated in an endowment ceremony. After spending some time in the celestial room, I still had not found the peace I was seeking; disappointed, I dressed and prepared to leave the temple.

As I walked through to the lobby, I saw standing against the wall a sister who had served me in the initiatory. Her face lit up when she saw me, and she eagerly gestured for me to come speak to her.

After expressing her joy at serving me that day, she uttered some of the most remarkable words I had ever heard. "When I was set apart as a temple worker," she told me, "I was promised that I would have revelation on behalf of the patrons I served. That happened today. The Lord wants you to know that the temple ceremonies were especially efficacious in your behalf today: you are clean every whit."

I walked away grateful beyond my ability to express for a Savior and a Heavenly Father who knew of my struggles and my doubts and who reached out to reassure me.

I had forgiven. It had been a long journey, and it had been a tremendous struggle. But in the end, I had forgiven.

And now I had *been forgiven.*

I had partaken "of the goodness of God,"[24] a goodness that is there for all who will make the choice and do the work to forgive.

23 Alma 11:43.
24 Jacob 1:7.

4
Healing, Thus Far, from Pornography and Sexual Addiction
Name Withheld

THERE WAS A SOUND.

Not the kind you can hear with your ears. It was a sound the heart makes. It was inaudible to everyone else and everything else. Only I could hear it. The sound of tearing and destruction—the sound of a broken heart.

It's a funny thing when your world falls apart when just ten minutes before you thought everything was okay. That was what happened to me. In one moment, my world collapsed, and my heart made the sound.

Two Weeks Before

I was sitting with Christine[25], a good friend of mine. We had been roommates for many years before I'd gotten married at thirty. We had experienced much of our single lives together. Christine hadn't married yet and was over at my house recounting her dating drama.

She told me how many guys she dated who had pornography issues. She felt like there was no way she was going to find someone who didn't have this addiction. Then she said, "You are so lucky Ben doesn't have this problem."

Then my heart did that crazy thing it always does when danger is near . . . the thing that happens when the Spirit is putting up a

25 Names have been changed.

red flag, waving it around to get my attention. I had had the inkling before, every once in a while through the years, but had kept sweeping it away.

At this point, Ben was working out of town a lot. He was gone for weeks at a time. So when I talked with him that night, I told him about my conversation with Christine. I asked him if he had ever had an issue with this. He basically said, "It's hard being a guy, for sure, but I'm okay."

I dismissed it. Left it at that.

Backstory

Ben was not a virgin when we got married. I was.

We met after he and his girlfriend had finished a relationship of about five years. I had moved to a new town for a work contract, and he had moved back to the same town to be closer to family after his breakup. It was then he decided to go back to church.

He had the classic Alma the Younger story: he went through a time of complete inactivity and rebellion . . . but when he came back, his testimony blew everyone else's out of the water. He'd had to dig deep to find Christ in his life, and it was obvious.

He'd had turbulent times in his life. Unlike Alma the Younger, he did not have a father who had taught him well. His mother had done her best to raise five children after her husband left because of extreme drinking, drugs, and immorality. Ben's father eventually committed suicide when Ben was only seventeen years old.

His mother worked constantly to keep food on the table for her five children. You can only imagine what the reality of daily life looked like. Turbulent. Stressful. Painful. Needless to say, Ben grew up with a lot of tragedy and loads of heartache.

We were set up on a date. I had never met anyone who treated me the way he did. I had dated a lot but had never been with anyone who adored me the way Ben did. He looked at me with adoring eyes. He fell for me whole heart and soul. He treated me amazingly. I wish I could describe how dynamic our relationship was. It was amazing.

We dated for a year. We got married. We had three kids. We met challenges. We lost a business. We tried again and again and had various successes. But through the seven years we were married, we had a passionate, devoted relationship.

Or at least that is what I believed it was.

Ground Zero

Two weeks after talking to Christine, I was tucking my kids into bed.

We called Ben since he was out of town and sang songs together—the same way we always did. We went through the regular bedtime routine.

But my heart did that crazy thing again. My gut lurched. When I saw him on the phone with the kids, I *knew* something was wrong.

Once the kids were settled in bed, I had the distinct impression to get on Ben's social media account. I am not a jealous wife. I never have been intimidated by much, especially in my relationship. I am not the kind of woman who "spies" to make sure everything is okay. I trust deeply. I worked hard before we were married to forgive Ben's past sins. I had succeeded.

But this night . . . this night was different. My heart was pounding before I even got on the computer. My chest felt like it was about to burst open. It was deafening to my ears.

After I signed on to his account, I immediately went to the messaging section. And there, before my eyes, was a live conversation he was having with his ex-girlfriend.

They were having cybersex. I had caught Ben having an online affair.

Everything slowed down. I remember looking at the screen and thinking, *This isn't real; this can't be real.* But I could see their conversation happening in real time right before my eyes. Pornography. Nude pictures. Horrific language. Things they missed. What they were feeling. What they were thinking. What they wanted to do. How they wanted to do it.

I read through it all. I scrolled back to see when this had started. They had been in communication for a few weeks. I had no idea whether they had seen each other in real life or not. But what did it matter? It was then that my heart made the sound. It broke. The love of my life was a complete stranger to me.

I picked up the phone. I called Ben.

"Hey, babe. You going to bed already?" he said. Like nothing was going on.

Silence for thirty seconds.

"I spied on you tonight. I can see everything you are doing right now."

Then I heard a sound—a whimper, a groan.

Silence for thirty seconds.

Online I could see him leaving the conversation. I could see her asking him where he'd gone.

"Jeanne . . ."

Now, anyone who knows me knows I don't come unglued easily. But something happened in that moment, and I snapped. I heard screaming. And it was coming from my body. I looked around the room, and it was shaking because my body was trembling so violently. Then it was like my spirit left my body, and I was floating in the air above. I could see from above the way I was reacting to him.

"I can't believe you would do this! How could you do this to me? To our children? To our family? How could you do this? Why would you do this?"

Then I came back to myself, zoomed down from my aerial viewpoint, and I was present again. And I told him I had to go. I had to go pray. And I hung up the phone.

The First Twenty-Four Hours

I'd told Ben I had to pray. And that is exactly what I did. As I hung up the phone, I realized I was already on the floor. I don't remember going there, but sometime during my meltdown I had liquefied, as if my body had no frame. I don't remember when the crying started, but by the time I crept to the couch in the next room, I realized my tears were gushing out like a waterfall.

I curled up in a ball on the floor and prayed without words. It was a prayer of my soul, reaching up to heaven for love, hope, reassurance, an understanding of what had just happened and who this stranger was. My body was aching, and I needed love.

Then Heavenly Father sent me an angel. My three-year-old daughter.

She came out of her room and said she'd been woken up and had to find me. She came to me and saw my tears, then rubbed them with her soft, chubby, toddler hands. "Mommy's hurt? Did you get hurt, Mommy?"

I sobbed, and I clung to her. In that moment, she was my nurturer. She was my support. She sat by me, and I put my head in her lap, and she patted my back and wiped my tears. We ended up going back to her room, and I crawled into bed with her.

I woke up an hour later from a horrible dream and made it to my room just in time for my body to start reacting. I ran to the bathroom and threw up everything I had in me. I threw up about five more times in the next twenty-four hours. I couldn't sleep. Every time I closed my eyes, I saw the horrific images and unbelievable language.

When the sun finally started showing through the clouds the next morning, I had a new understanding of those who stayed in bed all day long. That was what I did. I didn't get up. My three children under five woke up and came to me. I told them it was cartoon day, got them some easy breakfast, and went back to bed. I didn't sleep. I stayed in the fetal position.

I remember praying for an "*Ensign* moment." You know, those stories you read about in the *Ensign* where someone shows up at the door *right* at the pivotal moment they are needed most? I prayed for that to happen for me.

For someone to come.

For someone to call.

For someone to feel my heartache across the cosmos, to know I was important to someone.

Eventually the day passed. My body was grieving, my heart was broken, and my mind was numb. By nighttime, no one had come. My *Ensign* experience hadn't happened. I felt forgotten. I felt more alone than ever.

My Therapist

The Lord quickly became my therapist. Ben was due home seventy-two hours after the heartbreaking night. I got to work on my soul. In Alma, we learn about talking with the Lord about everything. The conversations in my head were 100 percent conversation back and forth with the Lord. No one had shown up for me, even when I had so badly wanted it, because the Lord didn't want me to reach out to someone else to process all of this. He wanted me to process it with Him and Him alone, without someone else involved.

I wrote in my journal. I wrote everything down. I wrote every question I'd ever had about our relationship. It all felt like a lie. I filled up three pages front and back with questions I had for Ben, which I was going to require him to answer for me. I prayed like crazy. I hibernated. I ended up hibernating for the next nine months of my life. I didn't want to pretend like everything was happy and normal, because it wasn't.

When Ben got home, it was like a stranger had entered the house. There were miles between us. The space was tangible. The silence was deafening.

The kids knew something was wrong because normally we were constantly talking and laughing together. Not now. Not this time. I remember looking at him and wondering who this man was that I'd married. *Who is he? How did he get into my life? What happened? Am I living a lie?*

Ben's Side . . . A Forgiveness Story for Myself

Well, now that you have heard Jeanne's side of the beginning of our journey, I am sure you want nothing to do with me.

Yes, this is Ben. Don't stop reading. You see, this is part of our journey—my forgiving myself.

I will start from the beginning of my sexual addiction. I was thirteen years old when I first saw pornography. I was at a sleepover with friends. A bunch of barely teenage guys got together, and, of course, it was the perfect time to prove our masculinity, so one of my friends got out a magazine.

The pictures I saw were intriguing. I knew it was bad to look at them, but my body wanted it, and I was curious. I wanted to keep looking.

The next chance I had was at my dad's house. As Jeanne mentioned, my dad had many problems of his own. Sexual addiction was one he struggled with. While I was sitting in the bathroom, I saw a magazine there. So I opened it. I looked at it. I wanted more.

Over the next five years before my mission, I kept my little secret from everyone. I was a shy kid. I didn't date. But I had fantasies, and the pornography problem grew. I felt amazing when I looked at these women and satisfied myself. And even though I knew it was wrong, I couldn't tell my mom. It was a problem, but I thought I could control it; isn't that what every addict feels? But I kept going. I kept looking. I liked it.

All during my teenage years, I ran to pornography to feel better. To feel better about myself. To feel better about my family. To cover up the pain that I was too immature to realize was so imbedded in my life. I'd raised myself—with a single mom and a dad who wasn't there for me.

When my dad committed suicide, pornography was a comfort for me.

But when I turned eighteen, I knew I needed to serve a mission. I knew I had to stop this habit. So I confessed. I went to the bishop. I told him. I stopped, and I got ready to serve. I went to Europe on my mission. There were still plenty of opportunities to keep up my addiction, but I stayed strong while serving. When I got home, I thought I could stay strong there too. I knew I could.

Then I started dating. I had never really dated before. Girls were actually liking me—they wanted to be around me. And it allowed something inside of me to blossom that hadn't been there before. Eventually I got into a relationship with a girl who was not a good influence. We dated for five years, and I ended up giving myself to her. She wanted it, and I wanted it. We continued in our sinful lifestyle for years, using a variety of sexual behaviors, even using porn.

But the whole time, I knew I couldn't marry her. I knew I had to return to the Church. I knew it two years before we actually broke up, but I'd gotten to a place where I was so far away from the Lord for so long that it was hard to take the necessary steps on what seemed like a steep, endlessly long staircase.

When we finally broke up after five years, I moved back to be closer to family and started going back to church.

I met Jeanne. She blew me away. I wanted to marry her the first time I saw her teach a Sunday School class in our ward. She was strong. She was amazing. She was full of light. And she was too good for me. Why would she want to be with someone like me? I avoided going out with her for quite a few months because I needed to heal.

Eventually my cousin set us up because he knew I had my eye on her. She was everything I had ever wanted in a wife. We dated for a year, and I couldn't believe she would actually want to be with me. I kept myself clean. I made it back to the temple. We were married.

It was about a year into our marriage when I started having whisperings to look at pornography again. We were going through some really stressful times with economics. I lost my business, we had to start over. . . and I allowed myself to indulge every couple of months again. Every time I was weak, I made a promise to myself to stop. I am sure Jeanne could feel the spiritual filth on me for days after.

I kept it a secret. I am really good at keeping secrets—every addict is until the addiction takes control of everything. The more stressful things were, the more I felt the trigger to indulge in pornography. I allowed myself to slip more and more.

But I didn't want to admit I had a sexual addiction.

Then I took a job out of town. I was gone for weeks at a time and was home for only five to eight days, then gone again. While I was out of town, I started indulging a lot. It got really bad. I would go home and be good while I was home. I would tell myself I had to stop, that I wouldn't do it again, but as soon as I was gone, the monster inside of me came out, and I became someone I didn't know. I became a carnal man . . . sensual and devilish.

Then I had an opportunity one night to have a conversation with my ex-girlfriend. It was exciting to talk to her again. I look at it now, and it was disgusting and unbelievable, but at the time, in the place I was in, I didn't care about anything but the excitement. I was fulfilling my lusts with pornography, but as with all addictions, I wanted more.

We started communicating and eventually had a sexual conversation. I kept asking myself why I was doing it. I promised myself when I woke up the next morning that I was never going to do it again.

But a week later, we had another one, and that was when Jeanne caught me.

I can't even say how grateful I am that the Spirit pushed her to interfere. It caused her a lot of pain to find out about my problems like that, but the Lord knew it was the best way for me to feel enough pain that I would realize I needed help. I was heading down a path that was going to cost me everything. Even now, talking about this, I am amazed it didn't cost me everything. I am so grateful she stepped in.

The next seventy-two hours until I was due home were excruciating for me. I prayed harder than I had in a long time. I couldn't believe I was back there again. I couldn't believe, when I stepped back to look at my life, that I had allowed pornography to lead me to such a black hole. Hadn't I gone through repentance before? But there I was, and I knew I had to get out of it to save my marriage, to save my life.

Jeanne and I didn't know how to handle such devastation in our relationship. Like she's shared, the silence was deafening the first time we saw each other after Ground Zero. I am just grateful she allowed me back into the house. She could have told me to go away. She could have told me she didn't want to see me. But she didn't.

Then, one morning about two days after I got home, we got up and made breakfast. It was a familiar routine, one we had done numerous times—I got the eggs, she cooked the waffles, I got the drinks, she set the table . . . . a seven-year-old system. But this time we weren't touching; we were avoiding each other. As I was at the stove making eggs, I suddenly felt her arms go around me, and she was hugging me and crying so hard. I crumpled at her touch and sobbed and cried too.

"Are we going to make it through this? How do we do this? Is this the end for us? How could this happen to us?" she said through the sobs.

"I am so sorry. Please forgive me. I am so sorry. Please forgive me," I said over and over. I turned around and held her.

Before she reached out to me, I knew I couldn't touch her. When she came to me and hugged me like that, she opened the door for healing and forgiveness. She was brave enough to let down the walls, and I was brave enough to respond and act.

I immediately scheduled an interview with the bishop. I confessed everything. The burden it took from my shoulders to not hide anymore was miraculous. At this point, I obviously couldn't go to the temple, *but I thought often about Adam and Eve after they had transgressed. Even after they had gone against the laws of God by eating the fruit, when they heard the voice of the Lord, they were happy, even excited to see Him.*

It wasn't until after *Satan pointed out their nakedness and told them to hide that they were afraid. It is the same with us. It has been the same with me. The Lord has always invited me to come out. He has called me so many times. "Ben . . . Ben . . . Ben, where art thou?" But I have listened to Satan—and hidden in the leaves and not come out—ashamed of my "fig leaf." Satan's power comes when we keep hiding and don't listen to the Lord's plea to come out and see Him. But Satan is bound when we do come out and repent because God is always there, His arms outstretched to embrace us.*

Navigating the oceanic depths of repentance was something I never thought I would have to do again. I knew what it was like to feel the "jaws of hell," as Alma the Younger described, and I'd never wanted to go back. But there I was, traveling that familiar road. Often during those first few weeks and months of working hard on my addiction, I related intimately with the words of Nephi:

> *Nevertheless, notwithstanding the great goodness of the Lord, in showing me his great and marvelous works, my heart exclaimeth: O wretched man that I am! Yea, my heart sorroweth because of my flesh; my soul grieveth because of mine iniquities. I am encompassed about, because of the temptations and the sins which do so easily beset me. And when I desire to rejoice, my heart groaneth because of my sins; nevertheless, I know in whom I have trusted. My God hath been my support; he hath led me through mine afflictions in the wilderness; and he hath preserved me upon the waters of the great deep. He hath filled me with his love, even unto the consuming of my flesh.*[26]

---

26 2 Nephi 4:17–21.

The sin that so easily beset me was sexual addiction. I felt "encompassed about," and many times when I wanted to rejoice, my heart groaned within me. But the Savior . . . He is so sweet. He is so powerful. His Atonement is real. I had and still have to work very hard to keep Him first in my life, but He has truly filled me with His love, which is all consuming. Because of that, I have forgiven myself and continue to do so every day.

I Will Not Deny the Christ

The Grand Canyon of emotions I felt over Ben that first week he was home was titanic. I felt such piercing anger that I wanted to throw him out and never see him again. I felt such great empathy and sympathy for the torment his soul must be experiencing that I wanted to wrap him in a never-ending hug. I felt such sadness for our future and had no idea if our marriage would eventually disintegrate that I wanted to keep him at arm's-length and just study him. I felt such perplexity about the conflicting emotions I was experiencing.

We were more candid than we had ever been during a conversation we had right before he went to see the bishop. I pelted him with questions about *everything* bothering me. He answered every single one, not once becoming defensive.

After he left to go out of town again (he worked out of town for four more months after this point), I went to see the bishop. He counseled and upheld me. He offered many suggestions for therapy, for help, for understanding, and for education on the subject.

Then he asked me a question. "Jeanne . . . are you going to make the choice to forgive?"

I had prayed and had already been working on my soul with Christ about this very question. I looked the bishop in the eye and said with conviction, "If I don't forgive, I will be denying Christ and the power of His Atonement . . . and, Bishop, I will not deny the Christ."

When adversity comes, the time for decision-making is over. My adversity had come, and I had made the decision years before

I'd ever met Ben about what the Atonement meant to me. My Savior is my best friend. We have been through hell and high water together. This new wilderness experience was not going to change that. Of course I would make the choice to forgive. Though I had no idea what the choice would mean in the everyday thrashing Satan inflicted upon my soul.

Spiritual Open-Heart Surgery

The process I went through in learning to forgive is best compared to open-heart surgery. My heart had been broken, torn apart. I needed some serious spiritual and emotional repair, and the Lord was my physician. He oversaw (and still does) the whole process. The Atonement and my Savior, Jesus Christ, were the tools, the thread, and the ultimate healing balm.

Yes, I made the choice to forgive early on, but that does not mean I went from loathing Ben one day to dancing and singing his praises the next. It was and still is a process. And it doesn't mean that going through *all* the peaks and valleys of the forgiveness process was (or is) easy. It's *hard* work. It's conscious work. It's down-and-dirty *real* work.

Inside Work

I hibernated from life. I truly did, just like someone does when they are in an operation—they are out cold while the doctor is working on them. That was me. I didn't talk to anyone I didn't have to. I stopped posting on social media. I stopped calling people. I stopped going out. I avoided friends. I stopped writing on my blog. I stopped painting. I stopped working on my business. Because I didn't want to be caught in a lie. I didn't want to have someone ask me how I was doing and have to look at them and say, "Not too bad." When in reality I was torn to shreds inside. I did as little as possible. My house was always a wreck. I didn't work on outside projects.

But while I was not accomplishing anything on the outside, I was busy with the Lord on the inside. I was on the operating table, the Lord working on my soul. That was where I was focused. I fell to my knees as often as I felt I needed to. I set my timer for every hour, and each hour, I would kneel and pray. I read scriptures. I slept. I put up a whiteboard in my bedroom, and *anytime* I had a question or a thought from Satan, I put it on one side of the board. When I had thoughts from the Spirit and the Lord, I put them on the other side. I did this daily, pulling out the weeds of anger, jealousy, fear, resentment, and hurt.

I wrote in my private journal like crazy. I cried anytime I felt like it. Ben made me promise that anytime I felt like I needed to express anything to him, I would call him and be open about everything. And I did. And he took it. He let me process and experience anything I needed to. He let me vent. He let me cry. He knew that in order for me to trust him again while I was doing this inside work with the Lord, I had to share it all with him. Feeling that willingness from him was one of the principal fruits of the Spirit in our relationship. And I started to trust him again.

The Temple

As I went through the forgiveness process, the temple became paramount. One of the many lessons I learned there came when Adam and Eve were denied the tree of life after they transgressed. The Lord protected the tree so they would not partake of the fruit and live in their sins forever.

If they had eaten the fruit immediately after they had transgressed, they would have lived forever in their sins because they would not have experienced their journey through the lone and dreary world, which was part of what actually sanctified them. It was *in* the lone and dreary world that they found repentance and forgiveness, and it wasn't because the Lord was by their side all the way. It was because they *actively sought the Lord.*

There were times when Adam sought for the Lord and for His answers, but Satan was *first* to respond . . . It wasn't the Lord jumping out of the heavens when Adam called on Him. Satan often stepped in first. He is always trying to block us from getting answers and peace from God. Adam could have been bitter and given up and said, "Lord, you aren't listening anyway, so I'll just give up and do what the world wants me to do."

But, no, he worked *hard* at his relationship with God while in the lone and dreary world. It was going through that wilderness experience that sanctified him to be ready to see the face of God again. It was by standing up for what he believed in, even when it was only Satan responding to him and not God. He said many times that he was looking for messengers from his Father. Adam would not stop trying until he received those messengers; he would not give up on the Lord.

This symbolism in regard to my process of forgiveness was key. I had experienced the harshness of someone else's sins. I was in the lone and dreary world for many months, wandering around, building my altars to God only to have Satan trying to interfere.

Too many times to count, I raised my arm to the square while I was in the car, in my room, in our home, or walking around with my kids to cast Satan out. He attacked me mercilessly. It was exhausting to actively remove the negative thoughts that sometimes plagued me *every moment* for months.

But I had made the choice to forgive. I would not remain a victim. If my marriage was going to fail, I promised myself it would *not* be because I had not worked as hard as I could to keep the Spirit with me, to let go of my anger, to let go of my fear, and to rebuild a relationship with my husband.

After many months of surgery, the Lord sewed me up. Yet everything still hurt. Anyone who has gone through surgery knows the aches and pains of rehabilitation. Learning how to move again and how to feel is a process. But the more you move, and the more you try, the easier it gets. It was the same with my heart and forgiving Ben. It ached a lot at first. My spiritual and emotional scar tissue ripped open quite a few times—sometimes from things he said, sometimes from when I took something the wrong way. And then there were times when I would question what he was doing with his time. But the more I focused on *my* heart and *my* mind instead of Ben's, the faster my heart healed.

Education

I sought constant learning. I have become an expert on the subject. I wanted and needed to understand all of this from a physical, mental, emotional, and spiritual point of view. I read everything I could get my hands on about the brain and the research that has been done.

I asked Ben to tell me what he was going through as well. He was open. He had made a promise to not hide from me anymore. We have come to have specific "verbiage" about it. We call it "The War" and "Daily Battles." I will ask him, "How is the war going?" And he can respond to me by saying, "I fought a hard battle today" or "I conquered today and never put my sword down."

Our Hearts Were Made Tender

After Joseph Smith was released from Liberty Jail, he said, "At length we regained our freedom and found refuge [in Illinois] . . . . We had suffered, but not in vain. Our hearts had been made more tender."[27] It is the same with Ben and me. Our suffering has not been in vain as our hearts have been made more tender.

It's like our relationship really started after all of this happened. The bishop told me several times, "If you work hard on this together, you will be stronger together than you can ever even conceive of now." He was right. I have to find a place of forgiveness for myself every day. Every day I have to forgive myself all over again—and not just for this sin but for my life and all my shortcomings. Every day I make the choice to put on the armor of God. The forgiveness and repentance process is not a one-time thing; it is an everyday choice to forgive myself and turn to the Savior for His perfect love to hold me up. Just like it's an everyday choice to love Jeanne, to respect her, to reverence her, to support her. Just like it's an everyday choice to stay committed to our relationship.

---

27 *Joseph Smith: The Prophet of the Restoration* (The Church of Jesus Christ of Latter-day Saints, video, accessed April 27, 2016, https://www.lds.org/media-library/video/2011-03-01-joseph-smith-the-prophet-of-the-restoration?lang=eng).

Going through this has caused me to look at all the ways I need to repent every single day. There is truly a war going on. Satan wants our marriage to fail. There have been plenty of moments and days in the past year and a half when I have allowed myself to blame Ben for everything. But to be successful, I have to look inside myself and see how I need to be more kind, more forgiving, more penitent, and more humble. It has been easier to heal when I keep my focus off of Ben and on myself.

I realized the times I was stuck in my emotions, because I buried myself with food. During the last year and a half, it has been easy for me to turn to food to feel good. Never in my life have I had a problem with overeating or binging. But now my heart is so tender toward anyone with a food addiction. They simply want to feel good. I have had to be very aware of how I cannot cover my emotional pain with food.

My heart is more tender toward those in marriages that fail. We have stayed together, but there are so many stories, so many different journeys, and not all of them have a good ending. Many end in sorrow and heartache—like my parents'. My heart is so tender toward my mom . . . but especially my dad. He allowed his addictions to overcome him and eventually take his life. My heart is so tender toward him, knowing perfectly the battle and work it takes to get past addictions.

I remember the first Sunday I went to church after everything came out. I wasn't listening to the speakers at all. I was sitting there looking around, thinking, *How many people here have problems I have no idea about? How many people are here not paying attention to anything because their life is crumbling to pieces?*

Everyone is fighting a battle. My heart is so tender toward those fighting private battles. There have been many times I've asked someone how they're doing and the Spirit has confirmed to me that they are fighting a battle no one knows about and that they won't talk about. I reach out and hug them as tightly as I can and show as much love as possible.

My heart is also more tender toward anyone who gets distracted from taking care of their repentance and forgiveness process. It is easy to get stuck inside life's problems—to be so overwhelmed and depressed by them that eventually, after time, you realize you haven't healed at all. Going through this journey has not been our only trial in the last year and a half. It has been accompanied by many other trials that were also hard to bear, including IRS invasion of our privacy and accounts, wages garnished, extended family needing support, unemployment, Mom in the hospital, etc. I felt so much pressure so often, I had to really concentrate hard on not shoving my repentance to the side. My heart is tender toward those who get stuck inside depression, loneliness, and anger, because it is easy to be stuck there.

My heart is tender toward those men and women whose companions don't choose to repent and who don't stay together. There were many times when Ben let me attack him with words and emotions. And he took it. He listened. He held me. He said he was sorry. He said he was changing. He meant it, and I knew it—"by their fruits ye shall know them."[28] Ben was sharing good fruit, fruit I could start building my trust on again. But my heart is so tender toward those who don't have this as a part of their story, as a part of their relationship.

Beautiful Heart Scars

I know someone who, years after undergoing open-heart surgery, has a visible scar on her chest. It is a symbol. It represents all the work it took to be healthy again and how much stronger she is today. "My heart works better than ever before!" she exclaims.

So does mine.

And so does Ben's.

And it's all because of the Miracle Worker, the Lord, our Perfect Physician, who made it possible through His Atonement. The Atonement of Christ helped me heal my sorrow and helped Ben heal his sin. We look at our scars now and how well our hearts have healed and are amazed at how well they are working.

---

28 3 Nephi 14:20.

The forgiveness process, thus far, has healed our hearts, and in the process, they have become even more intertwined than ever imagined. Now my heart makes a different sound of hope.

* * *

Two Years Later

Recently there was a death in our family. And because Ben's ex-girlfriend had been best friends with Ben's sister in high school, she was going to be there to help with part of the funeral planning.

When I found out, I had a bit of a meltdown. It actually surprised me how many emotions it brought up, especially because I'd felt like I had done so much inside work and Ben had done so much work to heal from his sexual addiction. When Ben understood the depth of the meltdown I was having, he had a hard time with it as well. It stirred up feelings inside of him like, "Doesn't she see how much I've been working?" and "It feels like no progress has been made at all." It was depressing for him as well as for me.

But a miracle happened. I had the opportunity to once again *really* turn myself over to Christ. I started repeating phrases in my mind like *Take this from me, Father. I can't do this alone,* and *Ben is Thy son, take him to your heart. Help me see him as you do,* and *Trust, forgive, and allow the Atonement to heal.*

Ben and I both worked, once *again,* very pointedly, on giving ourselves and each other to Christ. Forgiveness is a process—a constant process of giving ourselves to God.

Well, the day of the funeral came. The ex-girlfriend and I ended up seeing each other, even though we were both trying to avoid it. But the Lord was with me. When I saw her, I hugged her and said, "Thank you so much for all your work to help with this." She pulled away from me and said, "I can't believe you haven't hit me yet. You are a better woman than I am." I smiled at her and tried to open my mouth to say something, but she walked away.

I had been praying for my "enemy," and the Lord had softened my heart. I was able to let go of my feelings and give her to Christ as well. Forgiveness doesn't change the past, but it makes all the difference for the future. I don't know what our future holds. I don't know what mistakes I will make, what mistakes Ben will make. I can't control him. But I can control my heart, my peace of mind, and giving myself to Christ.

Recommended Study from Our Journey

1. *Becoming Spiritually Centered: And Overcoming the World,* by James Cox
2. *Leadership and Self-Deception,* by the Arbinger Institute
3. *Bonds That Make Us Free,* by C. Terry Warner
4. Sexual addiction reading list on LDS.org (so many resources here to dive into)
5. And, of course, last but certainly not least, the scriptures

There are many other resources, including the S.A. Lifeline Foundation, Fight the New Drug, and the Sons of Helaman LDS program. All can be found online.

Part III
PARENTHOOD

5
Everyday Forgiveness for a Perfectly Imperfect Mom

by Ganel-Lyn Condie

EIGHTEEN YEARS HAVE PASSED AT warp speed. All the grandmothers warned me that it would go by fast. My first baby is now six foot seven. As Cameron left for school today, I hugged him with my head resting on his chest. A lump grew in my throat as I sent him off into the world for another day.

Hugging him is like holding my own heart.

No more carpool. Cameron drives himself now. With fewer than three months till graduation, the yearbook staff wants me to send them photos. Don't they know what they are asking? It is dangerous work these days for this forty-five-year-old mommy to look through old photos. Each image from every stage of Cameron's eighteen years opens a floodgate of emotions: gratitude, regret, awe, guilt, longing, love, sadness, and joy. Nagging questions hang around like dusty old cobwebs clinging to the front-entry light.

Was I good enough? Did I mess him up with all of my mistakes and baggage? Is he ready for life? I pondered my myriad mommy mistakes as Cameron's old white Cadillac disappeared around the corner.

Tears inched out of the corners of my eyes as I offered a silent, secret prayer: "God, am I enough? Was I enough for this beautiful boy?"

New Mom

I became a mom on a stormy December evening in 1997. The hospital operating room was buzzing with activity.

After a seven-year journey with infertility, we were finally having a baby. It didn't seem to matter that Rob and I had taken an eight-week natural-childbirth class. I was now being wheeled into an operating room for an emergency C-section.

They always say (whoever *they* are) that being a parent changes everything.

When that ten-pound, dark-haired, gorgeous, crying baby boy was handed to me—everything did change! I remember whispering to him, "Cameron, it's Mommy. I love you. I am here. It is okay. I love you." Immediately my whole being was transformed. And he calmed.

We bonded right then on that cold operating table. I vowed to be the perfect mom, to sacrifice anything and give anything for this child. I was responsible for him . . . and mistakenly thought I was somehow in control of how his life would turn out.

That misunderstanding started back in the third grade. As a sensitive seven-year-old, I took an oath of perfection in the wake of my parents' divorce. They had separated when I was a toddler, way before Marie Osmond's first divorce, and I was the only one at Thursday Primary without a daddy at home. My angel mother had always tried her best to give us more than she had been given as a child. Mom would tell you herself that despite all her best efforts to get help, life was hard. Mistakes and mental illness meshed into some unhealthy family dynamics. That and the stress and heartache Mom felt leaked into our daily home life. She worked hard to do the best and to be the best she could for Meg and me, but life was uncertain. I was anxious and afraid much of the time.

Walking home from school one day, I felt the weight of the world on my seven-year-old shoulders. By then my mom had remarried a kindhearted man, but as it is in most blended families, life was sometimes challenging and tumultuous. I wanted more than anything to make things better for the people I loved. The sun shone brightly through the canopy of trees as I slowly dragged a stick along the fence. As the click-clack of the stick sounded against the posts, my spiritual eyes were opened, and I could feel God watching me. I had a sense that He had things for me to do, important things. Naively I swore to do them all and do them perfectly. I promised to be better and do better every day.

I committed to not let God down. I decided I didn't want to make mistakes. God wasn't asking me to be perfect, but the hope was that maybe I could change things, fix things, and create a safer life for my current family and the family I would hopefully have in the future. I pledged to marry the right person in the right place and create a peaceful, loving home for our children. I think future picket fences must have been part of the idyllic family image I'd painted upon my heart.

Peace and love became vitally important, like pure oxygen, because the contentious atmosphere at home felt suffocating. Somewhere in my immature and limited understanding, I had started to believe that making mistakes hurt people. I didn't want to ever hurt anyone. So when I made that pledge that day on the sidewalk, I also birthed a mental to-do list of how to be and what to do to protect everyone around me. I searched everywhere for ideas and answers regarding how to avoid causing pain and to live more peaceably. I watched and learned from other women, taking mental notes and making personal adjustments so I could fulfill my earthly mission with precision and honor. I wanted more than anything to be a conduit of God's love for those I loved.

So, long before studying and highlighting the *What to Expect When You Are Expecting* books of my cherished pregnancy, I had been formulating what I thought God expected me to be and do for my future children.

We brought Cameron home from the hospital, and within a few weeks, he was given a name and blessing in sacrament meeting. I took notes because I had to remember exactly what God wanted me to know about this precious boy. My heart was pricked when my husband spoke these words: "Cameron, you have chosen your mother because of what she will teach you." A bittersweet realization set in, and I felt panicked. Cameron seemed perfect, and I was, well . . . *so not*. How could I teach him all he needed to know for his amazing earthly mission when, after twenty-seven years of trying, I felt so inadequate and damaged? I hadn't been keeping up on my pledge as perfectly as I had hoped, and I didn't want to hurt or scare my little boy with my imperfections and ghosts.

The early stages of motherhood glow started to fade quickly into the background as a new understanding of what real exhaustion and sacrifice felt like. Fatigue seeped like a heavy paste into every joint and cell of my body. I fantasized about sleep. Really. If offered one million dollars or a night alone to sleep in a hotel room, I would have taken the hotel room.

I often cried along with baby Cameron during those 4:00 a.m. feedings. I prayed and pled with God nightly, "Please just help Cameron sleep." And then I'd wake from my few hours' sleep to dedicate my day to that little boy all over again. Bargaining with God, I thought that if I gave my all as Cameron's mom and did it all right, maybe it would be enough to make him happy, healthy, and safe. And somehow, if his childhood was perfect, the imperfections of my past would somehow be miraculously healed.

But I never really felt like I got to my all. I raised my voice in frustration more times than I want to remember, especially when his colicky crying wouldn't stop! My muscles would tighten as every nerve ending in my head seemed to be on fire. No matter what I told myself, it felt at times like his wailing would go on forever and that I would crumple from the tension. I would offer tired mommy apologies and more apologies to both Cameron and Rob for not doing it perfectly. My prayers were always to do better, to be better . . . tomorrow. But how?

It was painfully obvious that I was falling short of what I perceived to be the ideal and perfect mom. I panicked, thinking I was causing pain with my mistakes. Why wasn't I handling things better? Babies cry, and other mommies didn't freak out about it. I constantly scrambled and wondered if it was my fault Cameron wasn't more content and happy. The to-do lists swirled in my mind as I pondered and planned how to better nurse my baby, cook dinner, and get the laundry from the other side of the apartment complex back and folded before Rob got home.

At times nothing seemed to calm Cameron or me. I tried everything the book suggested, from bouncing him on my hip to strapping him into the baby carrier to running the vacuum. My nerves were shot, and my frequent anxiety led to mommy meltdowns. Those long nights and even longer days alone with my baby planted seeds of doubt that sprouted into major insecurities. Maybe I wasn't cut out for motherhood. No matter what I accomplished in a day, I felt like I had failed my baby and ultimately my God. I questioned whether the ghosts of my childhood were creeping into my new little family. But I was trying with every cell in my body to change old patterns, like my own courageous mother had tried to do and, I suppose, like every mother hopes to do to give her children more.

Life would never be just about me. From now on, it would always be about someone else too. This thought both terrified and exhilarated me. I had no concrete control over anything anymore. I could try to follow a nap and playtime schedule, but Cameron's moods or even getting out the door on time seemed dependent on a power bigger than me. My perfectionism went into hyperdrive in hopes of compensating for what I couldn't control. The simplest of tasks triggered anxiety: feedings, errands, appointments, and daily chores. They were small sparks setting off tension bombs inside my head.

School Mom

Diapers morphed into potty training—a process that almost broke Cameron's determined parents.

He learned to read at the age of three and was soon riding a bike without training wheels. Time was passing way too fast. I couldn't seem to keep up with this very active and intelligent little boy. Before I knew it, he was off to full-day kindergarten.

Where had all those playdates gone? I wondered why we hadn't done more Legos and chosen to worry less about getting the laundry done. I questioned myself a lot. Why hadn't I realized that having twelve Nerf guns really was the secret to a happy life? I still asked that same old question, "Have I already ruined Cameron's life with my own self-imposed expectations of perfection?"

Cameron now had homework, and we had a new baby in the house. With each new stewardship, my heart expanded—as did my self-imposed to-do list. I took it upon myself to take *everything* upon myself. I cringe when I think back on all those frustrating afternoons of trying to get spelling lists memorized and math papers completed before playtime. It wasn't Harvard. But I honestly feared that if I didn't make sure Cameron stayed up with his schoolwork, college wouldn't even be an option. Don't even talk to me about those science-fair projects and Cub Scout merit badges.

The daily pressure to keep up and check off the list took its toll.

The bewitching hours (from 3:30–5:30 p.m.) were the worst. Moms everywhere know what I am talking about. Homework needed doing, and dinner needed making. There never seemed to be enough energy or enough of me to get through to bedtime without losing my cool.

I remember a day sitting with my grade-schooler at the kitchen counter. I had prayed for patience just that morning, so I squared my shoulders and asked Cameron about his day. What I was really trying to do was get through his bag and help him finish the homework. Because it felt like my homework. Something to check off the list, signalling that all was well and that I had been a good mom that day. As I peppered him with questions about school, I prodded him to hurry and clean out his backpack. It felt like we were opening a secret-mission pouch with instructions for the day. What did the school want me to sign now? How had Cameron performed on the spelling test? Pulling out papers and bouncy balls, I grabbed a math assignment from the day before. We had worked so hard on it. So why was it still in his bag, ungraded?

My anxiety was on the rise as I questioned my restless son. "Cameron, why didn't you turn in your assignment?"

He didn't respond because he was distracted by his sister, Brooklyn, playing in the family room nearby.

Didn't the teachers know what this time of day was like? "Cameron, answer me. We worked on this. You need to turn in your work. It is your job to do your work, take it to school, and turn it in. Didn't you hear the teacher ask for it?"

"But she didn't ask for it," he replied.

Of course. His teacher was trying to instill a sense of personal responsibility, and the students were supposed to remember to put homework in the basket on her desk—with no reminders. Funny, I was trying to inspire that same characteristic in Cameron. And was failing!

"So why didn't you do it?" I asked.

"I don't know, Mom," came the answer.

I hated that answer. And I hated how I responded. Why was this such a big deal anyway? I didn't feel equipped to know if it was a big deal. Everything felt like a big deal because I didn't honestly know what would hurt or help Cameron in the long run.

I had no clear pattern to pull from.

All I knew was that his not turning in his homework somehow felt like my fault. Wasn't it my job to get my child to take responsibility for his own education? As his mom, I felt accountable for teaching, molding, helping, and controlling my child to become a reliable and dependable person. His teachers always told me how smart and kind he was at school. Wasn't that what would really matter later in life? But I feared that if he couldn't turn in his assignments, he wouldn't be a success, go to college, provide for a family, or keep a job.

I coached (lectured) Cameron a lot on being more conscientious and focused in class. I spoke firmly as my worry and nervousness crept into our daily conversations. Haunting questions tumbled around in my mind and heart: Which part was mine? What part was God's? And as my child grew, which part was Cameron's?

He was a loving, protective big brother. He was smart and funny. What more could I hope for? As I would kneel for my nightly prayers, returning and reporting to my Heavenly Father about the day, mistakes and missed opportunities would flood my mind. I hadn't cooked a healthy enough dinner. It was mac-n-cheese *again*. I had gotten too mad at the kids when they hadn't cleaned up the blocks by the piano after three reminders. Feelings of resentment toward my sweet and very busy accountant husband slithered around in my heart. Rob was working ninety-plus-hour work-weeks and doing his best. And I was flying solo on a route filled with unexpected turbulence. I was anxious and exhausted, and my kids repeatedly found me crouched and crying in the corner of the pantry. I was trying to hide my meltdowns so they wouldn't be scared by how out of control I felt. I didn't want them to ever feel fearful, especially of me.

The ghosts of the past whispered, *You are losing it. Your emotional baggage is going to ruin your kids. You can't make things better for them.* So, kneeling in prayer, I would again promise to do more and be more. "Forgive me for the mistakes of today. Help me forgive Rob for not meeting my needs. Forgive me for the hurt I have caused my family. Give me grace and wisdom to know what to worry about and what to let go of. Bless my children to be covered by the Atonement so my mistakes don't damage and hurt them."

Funny, my perfect Heavenly Father never lectured me about what I had forgotten to do that day or for crying in the closet. Each night the message from the Spirit squeezed through my limited understanding and regrets to whisper, *Just try again tomorrow.* The Savior was by my side, even as I felt the hope of providing a perfect childhood for Cameron and Brooklyn slip away day after day. God was trying to remind me that that wasn't part of His plan in the first place.

Raising Kids, Not Baking a Cake

As my son entered the teen phase, we enrolled in what I like to call the Advanced Placement Parenting Program. Reality hit—we really didn't know anything, but we were about to learn a lot about agency and mercy.

Cameron turned thirteen. We call that time the angry years. Fear and emotion pulsed through our home and family interactions. The tension was thick. Parenting a teen pushed us to our personal and emotional limits. Yelling and power struggles were so common with Cameron that each day I would wake up apprehensive about what would happen.

I not only doubted my husband's parenting approach during that time, but I also constantly questioned my own too. We were trying so hard to make things better for our kids, with more talking, less avoiding and yelling, but truthfully, we ended up raising our voices and slamming doors almost daily.

Then came the day Cameron took off after a heated argument with us. With no shoes. He had decided to run away. I can't even remember what specific issues had pushed us to the breaking point, though I do recall his disrespectful attitude and refusal to finish some school assignment. Since starting junior high, Cameron had had missing work more often and was failing classes. That had never happened before. He was constantly pushing against us, and we pushed back. We didn't recognize our son anymore.

The day he took off, sickness filled my gut. My hands were shaking as I started the car to go look for him. I drove and prayed until I finally found him. He was two miles away, walking along a busy road, carrying a bag of clothes. With semitrucks whizzing by, I pulled over and rolled down my window. "Cameron, please talk to me. Tell me why you are so angry lately. I don't understand why you're so upset. Why won't you just come home and do your schoolwork?"

As Cameron looked at me, I could see the hurt splattered across his face, and my heart softened. I told him I loved him and asked him if he wanted a ride. Calmer by this point, he said that he wanted to walk back by himself. As I drove away, I looked in my rearview mirror at my sad, confused, beautiful boy. Tears streamed down my face, and I wondered how we had gotten to this point and feared how bad it could still get.

What have I done wrong to cause this? This wasn't the happy, healthy family I had promised to have as a seven-year-old. If it was my fault, maybe I could fix it. So we tried everything from prayer to fasting to temple attendance to talking with professionals. I read books and tried to talk with Cameron about what was really going on inside. There was still a lot of love but not always a lot of liking, and things seemed to be getting worse, not better. The eruptions kept happening, and my unwelcome ghosts showed up more frequently.

I tried to keep our family struggles private because I didn't want to make it harder for Cameron to grow and change, but I couldn't always pretend and hide how contentious and volatile family life had become. When my visiting teacher came over, she listened, cried, and prayed with me. I shared what was going on with a few close friends but didn't want to talk about it with too many people for fear of gossip and judgment. I felt alone.

I prayed and cried out to God for help and strength. Something had to change, and fast, if our family was going to survive. Our innocent and happy Brooklyn was present and had to listen to the frequent fighting. I didn't want her traumatized by something she had no control over. She adored her big brother, and I wanted to protect that relationship from all the fear and contention. I wanted answers so I could fix it. Now!

One day, I was talking on the phone with a trusted friend from Boston about Cameron's struggles and what it had been like at home. She told me about a private school that offered a distance-education program. That conversation led to a profoundly clear prompting to try homeschooling Cameron. The decision was surprisingly easy to make, maybe because it was an obvious directive from the Spirit. It wasn't my idea because I had always said we would never—*no, never*—homeschool our children.

Cameron was definitely not happy at the public school, but we weren't sure why. He had told us about an issue with his old elementary school friends. Now he didn't seem to have a group to connect with. But could that really be what was causing the breakdowns at home? Maybe this change was the answer, at least for now. We called a family meeting, during which Rob and Cameron immediately agreed this was the right choice for our family.

Going forward on flimsy faith and totally uncertain about my own abilities, we enrolled him in Liahona's distance-education program for homeschoolers.[29] I was now going to be Cameron's teacher, and I became even more painfully aware of my flaws and more worried that my controlling nature and perfectionistic tendencies weren't all that homeschooling friendly. True, I had earned a teaching degree from Arizona State University (certified K–8) and had even once team taught fifty-two kindergartners in one classroom, but this felt bigger and scarier than anything I had ever taken on professionally.

Thankfully, the program gave us some much-needed support while I figured out this homeschooling thing. It was a real school, with live teachers and students, and was only forty minutes from our home. Cameron could go to campus sometimes to attend classes, but the majority of schooling would take place in our family room and kitchen. With a new desk set up by the couch, we seemed to have the best of both worlds.

But it was still a challenge. I felt like Nephi, who had been commanded to build a ship but didn't have any tools. So I tried to do as Nephi did, and I went back to the Lord often.[30] I woke each day and prayed, studied, and meditated. My husband and I went to the temple weekly. Sunrise always felt more hopeful than sunset. Inevitably, no matter how much I fasted and prayed in a week, Cameron and I still engaged in daily power struggles. Resentments erupted, and our mutual anxieties collided in heated conflicts.

So much about that time felt hard and overwhelming. I felt drained emotionally and ill-equipped to handle my teenage son's emotions. I often spent a portion of the school day in my walk-in closet, crying and praying. Pleadings to God seemed to be all I was sometimes capable of doing. I was lost. My son was hurting. My own inadequacies felt like a thick, suffocating smoke threatening to destroy my peace. Was there any hope for change and healing?

I called the school secretary so many times that year. Amy would always listen sympathetically to my concerns as I cried.

29 See www.liahonaeducation.com.
30 1 Nephi 18:1.

She would confidently reassure me I could do this and tell me Cameron would be fine. She was an angel God sent to help me trust myself and my son. Slowly I started to think we were going to be okay . . . someday.

As his teacher, I was responsible for his success. Or so I thought. Prodding him to get his work done, to study for the tests I had to administer, or to just focus long enough to get through that day's lessons became a constant power struggle. I often reflected on his baby blessing thirteen years earlier. I'd been promised that as Cameron's mother, I would and *could* teach him what he needed for his earthly mission. *But how, God?*

It felt like we were fighting a huge battle. Not just with each other but with Satan. After one emotionally charged conversation, I told Cameron he was going back to public school. I wasn't going to fight with him anymore. I was done with homeschooling. With thick mists of contention swirling all around us, we almost fell off the path that day—the path God had set us on. Crying, I called my husband at work. "I can't do it anymore. That's it! He resents me, and I don't know what to do. He won't listen. I can't help him, and I can't keep doing this."

Within moments of declaring the end of homeschooling for the Condie family, I felt a heavy darkness fill the room. I sensed the adversary laughing. In my mind's eye, I saw Satan. He thought he was winning! He wanted us to fight with each other—he loved contention![31] Satan wanted us to doubt the impressions and revelations that had already come from God via my friend in Boston.

Cameron was angry and emotional as he sat on the couch. "I don't want to go back to Millcreek Jr. High!"

It was in that moment that my spiritual eyes were opened. I could see the very real battle going on for Cameron's future and for our family. I could see what was being threatened. I stopped and took a deep breath, then stammered, "We aren't giving in to the fear and anger. Satan will not win. He doesn't want you to have this experience. He wants us to fight and give up. We will not give up on each other or give in." I knew that if God had led us to this

---

31 See 3 Nephi 11:29.

program, He would provide a way. Unseen blessings and learning had to be in store if we but steadfastly moved forward in faith.

As soon as I said we weren't going to give up, the darkness lifted, and the Spirit surrounded us. We cried and hugged. The adversary had lost this battle. But I knew he wouldn't stop trying.

From that day forward, when things got hard, I would remember what God had prompted us to do and how much Satan seemed to not want us to succeed. That thought would always strengthen me and encourage me to keep trying. Homeschooling didn't fix everything. But I knew if God had commanded it, He would provide a way. The scripture that often came to my heart and strengthened me was: "And it came to pass that I, Nephi [and Ganel-Lyn], said unto my father: I will go and do the things which the Lord hath commanded, for I know that the Lord giveth no commandments unto the children of men, save he shall prepare a way for them that they may accomplish the thing which he commandeth them."[32]

Looking back, I now see how many mistakes I made as Cameron's teacher and mom. I love schedules and thrive on routine, and homeschooling was often the opposite of predictable. It required a lot of daily forgiving and asking for forgiveness. Not many moms get to hang out with their teens during the school day. But the truth is, I sometimes longed for the time when Cameron was at school and I was able to take a well-needed break. Thankfully, as the days turned into weeks, hope and healing started to peek around the corner and out from under the spelling tests and math assignments.

Cameron gradually felt safe enough to start sharing in greater detail what had happened at Millcreek Jr. High. He had experienced bullying, and feelings of rejection from former friends had left him feeling socially unsafe at school. I cried with him and held him when he let me. Then I would go to my room and sob in private as I realized the hurt and confusion Cameron had been privately feeling. My mother's heart broke as I started to see a portion of what had contributed to the unravelling of my once-confident, happy son. Until then, he hadn't shared how bad it had been. He hadn't wanted us to know because he hadn't wanted us to rescue

---

32 1 Nephi 3:7.

him. Cameron stuffed the pain inside until it would explode in emotional outbursts at home.

I wondered how I had let this happen and what more I could have done to prepare him for the emotional land mines of junior high. Why hadn't he trusted us enough to tell us what had really gone on at school? Self-doubt washed over me as I recalled hours of orchestrating playdates, talking through social situations, and trying to model open family communication so my kids would *always* talk to me. I took responsibility for a lot of his pain—once again hoping that meant I could control the outcome.

Whatever oversights I had made or teaching opportunities I had missed, forgiveness seemed the only obvious pathway forward and out of the pain. Like Enos, I prayed for forgiveness for what I had done to add to his pain—for being too distracted and for not having all the answers. I prayed to forgive Cameron for the eruptions, outbursts, and drama he had brought into our home. And I prayed to forgive the bullies and friends who had abandoned him during this hormonally insecure time of life.

We tried to move forward, but it still wasn't perfect.

One day, Cameron was struggling to get through an English assignment. I can't remember the specifics now, but I wanted him to do something, and he certainly didn't see the value in doing it my way. I was frustrated and resented him and the situation. I *didn't* want to use my angry voice, but I wanted him to follow directions, be more obedient, and be more respectful. Eventually he got up from the kitchen counter and stormed back to his desk in the family room.

Fuming, I stood at the kitchen sink, gazing out the back window. The swing set was gently swaying in the autumn breeze, unlike my rapid heart rate pulsing angrily through my veins. I wondered if he would look back and cherish this time of his life or see it as a painful experience. I realized we sometimes acted like a couple of wounded, caged animals trapped together alone all day in the house, trying to get schoolwork done. I started to pray. I pled with God to help me with Cameron. I told my Father in Heaven how I really felt, how frustrated, resentful, and angry I felt trying to home-school. Then, silently, I asked how to communicate better with my child. A subtle, powerful answer came. Prompted by the Spirit, I asked in prayer, "Please, bless me with more charity. Help me love Cameron as Thou dost. I am willing to do it your way God, even though I don't know how." I ended the prayer and stood very still.

Then, as I turned back to look over at my beautiful boy sitting at his desk, I immediately felt the change begin. The gift of charity started to flow into my soul. My heart swelled with love as my anxiety started to crumble like the crisp fall leaves in the backyard. A heavenly wave of God's boundless love washed over me. In that moment, I saw Cameron as God saw him: smart and scared but still my loving boy.

I wasn't the perfect homeschool mom, but because of moments when God guided me and gave me the gift of charity, I managed. It wasn't *all* bad. I loved watching episodes of *Psych* with Cameron during lunchtime or sneaking off to go rock climbing or horseback riding for PE class. We drank a lot of Frescas, and I tried to enjoy a more relaxed school schedule. It was so obvious that home was where we both needed to be, at least for that one year, even though it wasn't always comfortable. It was the right choice at the right time for our son.

* * *

After one year of homeschooling, we decided Cameron would attend Liahona on campus instead of participating in the distance-education/homeschooling program. Honestly, I think we were both relieved with the change and break from each other. Once back at school, Cameron played sports and joined the drama team. He formed dear friendships. He felt safe to grow and learn and make mistakes. And in his senior year, he was even elected student-body president.

Six years have passed since Cameron's angry year, and he has progressed and developed in grand and beautiful ways. He has shared openly how the experiences of being bullied shaped and changed him for the better. But just like his mom, he is still a work in progress. Not finishing school projects until the night before they are due still happens, even in his senior year. Not turning in math assignments still seems to be an issue, but it can't be my fight anymore. This amazing young man must find his own path and overcome the obstacles placed before him.

Raising him has been both painful and joyful. Forgiveness, agency, and mercy are more important for all of us than I ever imagined during those seven years of infertility so long ago. Personal revelation has been key in making course corrections—even seventy times seven times.[33] Our experience is not a plug for private education over public. For our son, it was the right choice. With each of our parenting concerns, we tried to follow promptings, ask questions, and fast for additional revelation. We made the best decisions we could with the information we had at the time.

I still struggle to feel okay with his failures and mistakes because I am still struggling to understand that they are completely and totally his. I still feel responsible and afraid that maybe I didn't prepare him well enough for life beyond our kitchen table. I sometimes still wonder if I have fulfilled my promise to God.

The Savior Does the Saving and the Fixing

God keeps trying to teach me that I am not responsible for others' decisions or feelings. I can't prevent pain, even if I attempt to do everything right. Respecting someone's agency means learning to let go. My current season of motherhood, with an eighteen-year-old, is so much about stepping back and giving Cameron the space he needs to make his own choices. My husband and I have become more his advisers and aren't as in charge of his daily details. He is responsible for making his own mistakes as he struggles with real challenges and as he makes important life choices regarding college, a mission, and marriage. His great successes and missteps are between him and the Lord. These days, I am more on the sidelines and not so much on the field.

---

33 D&C 98:40.

For so long, I waited for a sense of relief and completion, a stamp of approval from God that my mommy to-do list was finally all checked off and completed with Cameron. I longed to take a deep sigh of relief and stop fearing that the ghosts of my past and inadequacies would sneak in and ruin his life. I didn't want Cameron or Brooklyn to feel unsettled or unsure. I wanted to know that I had been enough and done enough as a mother and wife and daughter of God and that He was pleased. But the outcome didn't belong to me. It belonged, ultimately, to God and to my children. As I said, I am still struggling to find what is mine and what is God's.

We will make mistakes! Individual ghosts have always been part of the plan—for each of us. That is why we were given a Savior. He is the Fixer, Finisher, and Great Mediator. God's everyday forgiveness in the plan of happiness is teaching me to let go, accept my own mistakes, and humbly persevere, yoked with the Savior.

Now, as we prepare to send Cameron out into the world, I cry happy tears over the smallest things. Everything during this last year has seemed to bring emotions to the surface: last swim party of the summer, last Christmas, and last Easter. Mothering from babyhood to childhood up through the teen years has formed a beautiful tapestry of both good and bad days. My view is a bit broader than it once was. The things that stressed me, that scared us as parents, no longer seem as important. God's mercy has helped me learn the business of raising a family. It will still take time, maybe an eternity, for me to become the parent God is, but I have greater faith that because of grace—not works—our family will be okay.

I love watching my boy grow into a man.

He has his own faith and ideas about how to make the world a better place. He has taught me to relax and laugh more. We share a love of politics, classic rock, and the Savior. He is strong, brave, honest, and tenderhearted. And he is still becoming. I know it's time to step out of the way and let him figure out how the rest of his life is going to go.

Motherhood requires a lot of doing and trying and fixing. But just like a doctor who can't always prevent disease or save every patient, I have to stop trying to be and do it all. The seven-year-old inside me falsely clings to that standard of perfection, but I am learning to move forward steadfastly in faith, daily repenting and trusting in God's power more than in my own. I am also learning to forgive my own shortcomings.

It isn't my job to fix everyone. But I can testify of the source Cameron can turn to when he falls short and fails. Neither one of us will be perfect, and we may even cause pain for others. And that is okay. The Father knew that only through the Atonement of Christ, all ghosts—both past and present—would be conquered.

When I think of my dedicated mother, I feel love. I know her flaws and forgive her. My prayer for my children, maybe when they become parents, is that they will forgive me as they look back at my mistakes. I'm sure they will remember some of my wrongs, but I hope they will mostly see my unending love.

That is how I choose to see my parents.

Recently, Cameron was leaving the house to hang out with friends on a Saturday night, but before he left the kitchen, he stopped and said, "Mom and Dad, I don't think I have ever said I am sorry for the angry years. I've wanted to, but I just haven't. I am sorry for how I was."

I started to cry. In return, I said, "Cameron, thank you for apologizing. But we need to say thank you for allowing us to learn and grow along with you during that time. We became better parents because of that experience. Please forgive us for the mistakes we've made. We have already forgiven you."

In the kitchen that night, as I watched Cameron drive away in his old white Cadillac, I saw the beauty of *everyday forgiveness.* Pictures from the scrapbook of his life and my own flitted across my memory. Christ's mercy had molded our messes into cherished masterpieces!

I am grateful for the lessons we have both learned and will continue to learn along the way. I didn't have to do everything perfectly. I just had to have a willing mother's heart and forgive myself and my son for our shortcomings. Most importantly, I had to stay close enough to God to receive His unconditional love.

6
Daddy Didn't Want Me
by Marie Marjorie Labbe (Stage name: Marj Desius)

I FEEL LIKE I HAVE been fighting for life since before life began.

My family lived in a small town in Haiti—Croix Des Bouquet. It was a small village where people survived mostly on home-grown food and managing their own little piece of land. If they didn't own property on which to build their own place, they were considered really poor. My parents were staying in a small house that belonged to my grandmother at the time. It was normal in our culture for parents to help their children when they were just starting out.

One evening in early September 1983, my mother accidentally conceived a baby.

It was six weeks later, after missing her period, that she realized she was with child. She was worried about telling my father since they already had a three-year-old boy. My parents didn't have the best relationship at the time. The fighting was constant, as were the financial struggles. So Mother hid her pregnancy for a couple weeks. She was worried about being able to take care of my big brother and me, but she knew she wanted to keep me, so she decided to tell Dad the truth.

He was not happy! It was the early eighties, and as I said, my parents were under great financial stress. They were already struggling to take care of their little boy and pay for the basic necessities of life.

News of another child coming was bad news. Dad wanted Mom to get an abortion. In my country, that was legal. People who wanted to end their pregnancies usually went to a midwife for help. Some used natural herbs at home, but at their own risk. Mom refused. She already felt a love for me, even though I was unborn. So she made the decision to keep me and fight to have me.

She made it clear to my dad that she was going to have me whether he wanted me or not. I guess she made him accept the decision as time went on, but it didn't help their relationship.

* * *

My dad was a tailor and made suits for a living. My family depended on his business for all our basic needs. If he did not sell a pair of pants or someone did not come to have a suit fixed, he didn't make any money for the day. His income was based on his daily prayers that someone would come into his little shop for one thing or another. Dad didn't have a big operation, and he never made a lot of money, but he made enough to feed us.

* * *

During the pregnancy, Dad once again put his foot down—he did not think I should live. Knowing this, I felt unwanted, like I was a mistake.

One day, my father even tricked my mother and secretly put some strong herbs in her tea, attempting to induce a miscarriage. She unknowingly drank the concoction. Later he confessed to what he had so maliciously done, and my mother prayed and faithfully believed that somehow I would be okay.

She held on to that faith, and I was born on June 5, 1984—a healthy, strong, and perfect baby.

Daddy was there for the first six years of my life. No matter what his feelings were for me, I loved him so much. Mom said he eventually grew to love me. He tried his best to take care of our family, but one day the pressure became too much. I was young, but I clearly remember the day he left us.

I kept thinking it was for a short time, that he was coming back for us. Sadly, that was not the case.

* * *

It has been more than twenty years now since I have seen Dad.

He'd left for good. At times he would send money to help my mother with expenses. He tried to stay connected via sporadic phone conversations, but it wasn't enough. The reality was that I didn't have a father in my life.

Like any child, I wished my dad had wanted me and wanted to be there for us as my mom struggled to raise us. I wanted a dad who played hide-and-seek, who taught me how to ride a bike, and who gave me advice when I made bad choices. I was heartbroken that he had left, run away from the daily struggle, and that Mom had to do it alone.

I didn't resent my father, even though I knew he never wanted me. But it was still hard. Growing up without a dad felt like growing up in a jungle without much protection. The money he sent didn't mean much to me at the time. I wished he would ask how we were doing or talk to us. I needed a friend and an example.

I wanted a hero, a protector.

Six years after my dad left, a gang broke into our home in the middle of the night and took everything we had. One of the gang members pointed a gun at my brother's head while another one pushed me to the floor and tried to rape me. My mother screamed and begged them to leave me alone. Then the gang members started to argue among themselves, and one said, "Leave her alone. They gave us all they had. It's time to go to the next house." Miraculously, they let my brother and me go.

After this traumatic experience, I became paranoid, afraid to walk in the streets alone and so very scared of the dark. I had hallucinations that people were following me, and Dad didn't even care. I blamed all of these traumatic experiences on him—because he wasn't there. He wasn't there to protect us or prevent things from happening like a father should be.

I began to hate him. The pain in my heart was so intense. If he'd been around, maybe I'd have been safer, I would have believed in myself more, and I could have believed and trusted others as well. I wanted a heroic father—not just my heroic mother.

In my early twenties, however, I began to think of my father in a different way. I started to feel compassion for him and tried to reach out to him. I called to find out how he was doing. Our conversations were short, and he didn't ever open up or acknowledge the hole he had left in our lives.

As I've gone through my own process of repentance and forgiveness, I have felt the power of the Atonement. I am not trying to make excuses for my dad, but through the Spirit, I started to see how scared, confused, and lost he felt. I came to understand that he had treated us the way he felt about himself. He didn't have the capacity to care for a family.

* * *

I became a member of the Church March 28, 2009. My conversion taught me a lot about forgiveness. I learned that God loves His children no matter what. He loves me no matter what I have done or who else loves me. My thoughts about my dad and the pain he caused continued to shift. Through the Spirit, I came to better understand how my dad felt and that he was in a dark place. I saw how he'd had no way of taking care of us and had gotten scared and how his guilt had driven him away.

Still, I fought with these spiritual insights and promptings. I wanted answers. Why did he never like me? How could he not want me to even be born despite the circumstances?

Becoming a follower of Christ, I started to change and become someone who cared less about what people did to me and more about what I did for others. I became more compassionate and aware that God loves all of His imperfect children.

I started to forgive my dad because I began to see that the Savior loved him, and in spite of everything that had happened, I loved him too. I wanted to move forward, so I decided to stop beating myself up and stop judging him. There was hope, even without a father. And with the Savior, there could be healing.

I hope one day my dad will come to understand the real meaning of family. Family means we struggle together, we face life together, we don't give up. My prayers have continued every day that someday his heart will change as mine has. That he will find peace, as his loss may be even greater than my own.

* * *

Now I am a mother. Becoming a parent has opened my heart, and even more, I want to forgive and help others to heal.

Sometimes God sends children to families who want them from the beginning, families who cherish them. Other children are born into difficult situations. They, like me, must often literally fight for their lives.

I am stronger than I was yesterday. I hated growing up thinking I was a mistake. But today I don't allow this pain to control my thinking or my life anymore. I don't hold any anger or hatred toward my dad. I forgave him, even though he didn't ask for it. When I get a chance to talk to him on the phone, I tell him I miss him. I tell him I want to come see him, wherever he is.

I have learned that how my father treats me says more about who he is than who I am. I hold a testimony in my heart of God's love for me. As my Heavenly Father, He wants me to feel His pure love. It has powerfully overcome the lack of love I have felt from my earthly father. When I became a follower of Christ, the door was opened to choosing compassion instead of hurt. I realized how much God loved the person who hurt me. I forgave my dad because I loved him and chose to stop judging him. In some small way, I want to show him there is hope, that he too can be healed from the past.

Today I am a wife who is trying her best, a mom with a full heart, and a true friend who enjoys hugs and laughing with others. Learning to forgive has helped me breathe. Like that first breath I fought to take as I came into this world, I have fought for forgiveness.

The consequences of thirty years of abandonment and the terrible mistakes I've made along the way may not be erased in this lifetime, but God has whispered to my heart that every loss can be restored through the Atonement of Christ.

All pain will be paid for, and all hurt will be healed, for I have a Father who has always wanted me and will never abandon me.

Part IV
SEXUAL ABUSE

7
"O That I Were an Angel": A Story of Sexual Abuse and Forgiveness
by Barbara Skovensky

"O that I were an angel, and could have the wish of mine heart."
—Alma 29:1

I TRULY DO WISH THAT I were an angel and could speak with the trump of God to teach all about the Atonement and love of Jesus Christ, our Savior and Redeemer. If anything good can come from experiences like mine, sharing the healing power of the Atonement and the love of God are two of them. I've found there is healing in sharing the story of my abuse and recovery. My message is one of hope, renewal, and forgiveness. My testimony is of the peace, trust, and hope that come to all when they seek healing through the power of the Atonement of Jesus Christ. My desire now is to be an instrument in the Lord's hands in helping others who may be silently suffering the effects of abuse.

I was a victim of multiple incidents of sexual molestation, starting in my early teens. I was fourteen at the time and had grown up sheltered and unaware of people with bad intentions. I was extremely trusting and was a people pleaser. I wanted to make everyone happy.

From my clearest recollection, there were six men who, on separate occasions (sometimes in multiple encounters), violated me sexually. Several of the men were of some prestige in the community.

Some were members of my branch in the Church. They were all people I had known and trusted.

But they violated that trust, and I became a victim of an abuse that began in the dark and in secret and occurred over a two-year period.

The first incident was in an airport. My family was waiting in the airport's military lounge for our flight to Turkey, where my dad was to serve for two years.

I only remember bits and pieces of this first incident. I was in an enclosed area with a young military man, who was probably in his early twenties. He was being stationed in Turkey too. I don't remember how he managed to get me alone with him, but I remember how terrified I was when he started kissing me and touching me inappropriately. Frightened and having no idea what to do, I became as still as a statue, praying that the molestation would soon end and that I could escape.

The next time was on a bus going from Incirlik, Turkey, to Ankara, Turkey, for a cross-country track meet. I was sitting next to a senior student I didn't know very well. It was late and cold, so I had a blanket over me, and I drifted off to sleep on the dark bus. I was awakened by someone touching me, and realized I was being molested, even with my father on the bus as a chaperone. Again, I did not know what to do so I pretended to be asleep. I felt dirty and ashamed, so I never told anyone what had happened.

The next abuse experience involved a neighbor. He was married and was a young father. My brother and I would go across the street to hang out with him. I remember he had a cool car he let us both drive and was a police officer on the air force base where we lived.

One day, he followed me to a babysitting job. He had me pinned on the couch when the parents came home early. For so many reasons, this was a tragic event for me. But looking back, it may have been a blessing in disguise because it stopped his actions before they escalated.

My parents were called. The police were called. I was sent home.

I remember being upstairs in my room all alone while my parents spoke to the police. No one spoke to me about the incident, *ever.* I felt like a bad girl—so bad that no one would talk to me. I felt so alone. I felt like the situation I had found myself in was entirely my fault. The only people who ever talked to me about what was happening were the abusers, and they were in positions of authority, so I believed them. They would say things like "If you weren't so beautiful, I could control myself" and "Pleasuring men is all you're good for." These distorted thoughts ran through my mind over and over. Since the abuse continued to happen, I believed what these men were telling me, even though I was trying to do everything I could to avoid being abused. My self-esteem plummeted as Satan continued to whisper lies.

The neighbor was forbidden to speak to me again. I would still see him riding around in his patrol car, watching me, as I walked to school. I was always frightened that he would try to get me alone again. Thankfully he never did.

The other experiences were similar—men who could not help themselves because of my beauty, according to them.

Feeling worthless, I believed overwhelmingly that Heavenly Father could never love me now. Feelings of guilt and shame filled my heart and mind. Because of what the abusers had told me, I felt like I deserved what was happening to me. These men had said they couldn't help themselves around me. I was too young to recognize the lies for what they were—with childlike innocence, I believed them. I was so naive and trusting; they were the adults.

Who could I talk with about the abuse? Anyone? Even though my parents knew about the police officer, they remained silent. Following their lead, I felt it was a dirty little secret I had to keep hidden at all cost. In time, I learned more about how secrecy feeds the feelings of shame that come with abuse. That shame was something I would carry for years.

I eventually married a loving and patient man. Intimacy within our marriage was rocky. I do not remember when I finally found the courage to tell him about the abuse; it was early on in our marriage though. He was angry that I had been hurt and that he had not been able to help me. I told him I felt broken. There were times I didn't want to be touched, and he would feel unloved. I had trouble separating the beautiful intimate relationship I had with my husband from the feelings of shame I carried from the abuse. Because of my husband's patience, I have been able to work through these challenges as I have grown to love myself more and forgive myself, and now I enjoy the intimacy we share.

* * *

It was terribly difficult for me to forgive myself. It has been a long healing process—twenty-five years—and I cannot say for sure that it is totally complete. Healing takes time, but I believe we can be healed.

One of the first things that helped me understand that while I was not responsible for the abuse, I was responsible for who I chose to be from here on out was a set of motivational tapes my boss at the time had purchased. I would listen to these tapes while I worked. One of the first principles I learned was that when you cast yourself in a victim role, someone else is always the cause of your problems. Playing the role of victim, you have no power to change the things around you. I decided I no longer wanted to be a victim. That meant taking responsibility for how I was thinking and feeling and choosing to let go of my wounded-little-girl identity. It was a shift in perspective that served me well. I could now see a glimpse of hope.

Eventually, I started to feel stronger and like I should share my experiences with one particular friend at work. She had been open with me, so I felt pretty safe, but I was still scared. Questions swirled in my mind: What would she think of me? Would she think I was horrible and repulsive? Would she think I was loose? Unworthy? Would she still want to be my friend? I was relieved when she reacted with kindness and empathy. This experience gave me courage to share again, but not for some time. As I shared my story, I became stronger. I no longer lived in the shadow of secrets and lies. I was taking back my power.

During my first pregnancy, I finally got up the courage to go speak with my bishop. I had learned early on in my abuse that I could not trust adults, particularly men and police. I could not even trust my parents, so going to the bishop after I had already been married in the temple was scary. But I had come to realize I could not live with this secret anymore. I was still blaming myself for the abuse. I felt I needed to be punished for what I had done, but I trusted that the Lord would deal fairly with me. I was desperate to confess so that I could, with a clear conscience and lighter heart, move on in raising this beautiful baby Heavenly Father had blessed me with.

I humbly went in to my bishop, feeling in my heart that I might even be excommunicated. I had accepted even this so that I could eventually enjoy the freedom of complete forgiveness. Fortunately, my bishop was close to the Spirit. He could see my pain as I spoke of the abuse. He prayed with me and told me he felt that I was clean in the eyes of Heavenly Father and the Lord. He renewed my temple recommend. I went away from that interview feeling comforted but not entirely clean. I was so hard on myself. I did, however, allow myself to feel the Christlike love of this bishop. I believed He was close to Heavenly Father and I could trust him. He believed I was forgiven. I wanted to believe it too. It was in this moment that my heart was opened to forgiving myself.

It was another seven years after meeting with the bishop when I gained a clearer understanding of the Atonement and the Savior's role in my healing process. As I was pondering one day, feeling lost and alone, I randomly opened my general conference magazine to a talk President Thomas S. Monson gave during the priesthood session in October 2002. My eyes fell upon the words to the hymn "Master the Tempest Is Raging":

Master, the tempest is raging!
The billows are tossing high!
The sky is o'ershadowed with blackness.
No shelter or help is nigh.
Carest thou not that we perish?
How canst thou lie asleep
When each moment so madly is threat'ning
A grave in the angry deep?

And then the assuring chorus:

The winds and the waves shall obey thy will:
Peace, be still.
Whether the wrath of the storm-tossed sea
Or demons or men or whatever it be,
No waters can swallow the ship where lies
The Master of ocean and earth and skies.
They all shall sweetly obey thy will:
Peace, be still; peace, be still.
They all shall sweetly obey thy will:
Peace, peace, be still.[34]

I do not believe I even read the rest of the talk. The words to this hymn were the answer to my unspoken prayer. I had felt over-shadowed with the blackness of the abuse. The stories of the past were my constant companions. I had allowed them to define me—a secret part of me only a few knew about—but at this moment, the words to this song gave me peace. The Spirit whispered that as I kept Jesus Christ with me, nothing could swallow me up.

Knowing this truth and allowing it to become part of *my* truth were two very different things. I was healing, but it was coming at a comfortable pace for me.

The next step in healing was recognizing that I was in a wilderness of my own making. This truth came to me when a friend and mentor invited me to read Exodus 16, which tells the story of the children of Israel being lost in the wilderness. By their own choices, even though they may not have realized that it was their disobedience and fear that kept them in the wilderness, the Israelites wandered for forty years. God had not left them. He was blessing them with manna from heaven every day the whole time they wandered. As I read this story, the Spirit witnessed to me that I had kept myself lost in my own wilderness of the past, in my "victimhood." I gained a deeper understanding of how I did not need to stay a victim, of how I was in control of my life.

---

34 *Hymns*, no. 105.

I was blessed daily by my loving Heavenly Father, and I often saw those blessings, but because of my refusal to let go of the past and because I could not forgive myself, I was unintentionally rejecting my Savior's beautiful Atonement. The problem was I didn't know how the Savior could forgive me. Sexual sin was one of the greatest sins, and despite that bishop's assurance and all I had learned, I still believed deep down that it was my fault. I yearned to be free of this burden but didn't know how it could be done. Then I read, "Come unto me, all ye that . . . are heavy laden, and I will give you rest" (Matthew 11:28). And in 3 Nephi 9, I found another comforting scripture: "Behold, mine arm of mercy is extended towards you, and whosoever will come, him will I receive; and blessed are those who come unto me" (v. 14).

In the beginning of my experiences with abuse and through years of holding on to my pain, I told myself, "You should have known better." "You should have stopped it." "Why did you let this happen?" And all the while, the Savior was saying, "Come unto me, [Barbara], and I will give you rest." "Come unto me." Instead of giving myself and my burdens to the Savior, I was either constantly punishing myself or trying to be good enough to prove my worth and essentially save myself that I could not see the hand of the Lord extended toward me. I knew logically that Jesus loved me; I just didn't feel worthy of that love, so I kept trying to prove myself.

I had to let go of the illusion that I could fix this. I had to choose to trust in God and the power of the Atonement. I had to believe that Christ died for me and that through Him, I was always good enough because He would make up the difference between what I could offer and what was expected. It is through Christ that I can make the declaration: "I am perfect, whole, and complete." As I actively choose to follow Christ, I truly am perfect, whole, and complete. He makes everything right.

As I look back on the past, I realize that with the knowledge I had at that time, I could not have chosen any differently. Certainly, with the experience, light, and knowledge I now have, I can look back and see things I might have done differently, things I wish I would have done differently. But I cannot go back. The past happened, and rehashing the details will not change it. So with time, and being guided daily by the Spirit as I did my part to stay close to Him—reading my scriptures, saying my prayers, attending church, going to the temple, and keeping my covenants—I chose to love that fourteen-year-old girl. I would stand in front of the mirror and look into my eyes and say, "I know you did the best you could. I forgive you for what I believe you could have done better, and I love you." It took a lot of effort. I cried often, but I eventually came to love myself.

I know today that I am a daughter of a loving Heavenly Father. I acknowledge that something tragic happened to me, but I've decided I'm not broken and I don't want to be a victim. If I believe I'm a victim, I rob myself of the power to change and have a better life. By choosing to remain a victim of the thoughts and experiences of the past, I abuse myself.

Through the love of my very supportive, kind, loving husband, wonderful children, family, leaders, and close friends, I chose to separate my individual worth from those terrible experiences. I chose to obey Heavenly Father's command: "Judge not, that ye be not judged."[35] I realized it was sinful for me to judge even myself. And it was not good in any way to separate myself from Jesus Christ and His atoning sacrifice. He suffered for me, even before I suffered. He knows my pain. He already paid the price. He understands me completely.

In preparation for writing my story, I finally shared the details of the abuse with my parents. We had never spoken about it, so when we did, they were understandably sorrowful. Since then, they have been supportive and grateful that I came through these experiences a stronger person. My mom has even said that I am her hero.

I am still healing. Very recently, I was reading my patriarchal blessing, which contains a couple of sentences that have always bothered me. These sentences reinforce what I said to myself as a victim: "You are a beautiful young lady, and you will grow to maturity as a

---

35 Matthew 7:1.

beautiful woman. Many men will be attracted to you. Do not be deceived." I had always read this as a warning, and it had been a constant reminder of the abuse, so I had a difficult time reading my blessing because of it.

But when I read it this time, I felt a prompting to go to my bishop to ask for an addendum to my patriarchal blessing. My bishop had only been recently called, and he sought direction from the patriarch. It was difficult for me to tell the bishop my story and share these sentences from my blessing and the concerns of my heart, which surprised me because I felt like I had put these experiences behind me. But the bishop was so empathetic. He listened with his whole heart and was sad to have to tell me that the only reason they would make an addendum to someone's patriarchal blessing was if the lineage had been left off. My heart was heavy, and I wondered why I had been brought to the bishop's office only to be turned away. He left me with kind counsel and a priesthood blessing, but I felt confused.

As I left his office and headed down the hallway toward the exit, I ran into one of my best friends. She could tell I was upset, and I shared what had happened. She said, "You are a beautiful woman. Many people—men and women—will be attracted to you and your light." All of a sudden, through her eyes, those sentences in my blessing were reframed. They were no longer negative and ugly. My trip to the church had become a gift. I finally saw that Heavenly Father sees the beauty in me—not just my physical beauty but the whole me. Also, I learned that I am still learning, growing, trusting, and letting go of the past.

I have come to know that even though bad things happen to good people, there is hope in and through the Savior, Jesus Christ. He loves us. Unwanted as these experiences were, I have been humbled and refined through them. I know my Heavenly Father and Savior better than I knew Them before. I am grateful for the gift of the Holy Ghost and His comfort and constant companionship. I have immense gratitude in my heart for the great plan of happiness and for the Atonement, without which we would all be lost.

For anyone who has suffered *any* kind of abuse in silence, please have the courage to tell someone. Reach out. We were never meant to suffer alone. Once shared, a secret loses its power to keep you a victim and makes room for hope and healing.

My burdens have become blessings because in healing from these experiences, I have developed gifts that allow me to help others. I have compassion for others' suffering. It has not been an easy journey, but I am grateful to be in a place now where I can see how Heavenly Father has blessed me all along. I am grateful for who I have become through the Atonement and for the deep and abiding testimony I have gained of Jesus Christ. I have learned for myself that it is not enough to believe in the Savior; we must *believe* Him. He can and will do all He has said He would do. As stated in Proverbs, we must "trust in the Lord with all [our] heart; and lean not unto [our] own understanding." If we acknowledge Him in all our ways, He will direct our path.[36] When the Lord says, "Behold, your sins are forgiven you; you are clean before me; therefore, lift up your heads and rejoice,"[37] He means it. I trust that I have been forgiven. This knowledge allows me to keep living each day with peace and hope. The Atonement is real. Heavenly Father and Jesus Christ really do love us and have provided a way for us to overcome adversity and challenges.

I do not understand why abuse is allowed to happen, but I do have a testimony that Heavenly Father is very aware of each of us. He will help us navigate the obstacles that come into our lives. He will carry us when we are weak. He will comfort us as only He can. He will sustain us, and He will deliver us!

Forgiveness is a gift and a process. It starts with a desire to want to forgive. I have been able to forgive myself for thinking that I should have known better or that I somehow could have stopped the abuse or protected myself from what happened. I have been able to forgive my parents for not showing up for me the way I wished they would have as I went through these ex- periences. And I have been able to forgive the men who abused

---

36 Proverbs 3:5–6.
37 D&C 110:5.

me. The Lord commands us: "Wherefore, I say unto you, that ye ought to forgive one another; for he that forgiveth not his brother his trespasses standeth condemned before the Lord; for there remaineth in him the greater sin. I, the Lord, will forgive whom I will forgive, but of you it is required to forgive all men."[38]

I am grateful we are commanded to forgive.

Everyone needs the Atonement of Jesus Christ.

---

38 D&C 64:9–10.

8

Left Behind: A Journey of Forgiveness after Sexual Assault

by Bonnie Larsen

MEMORY IS AMAZING; WHEN WE focus on something that happened years ago, we can begin to relive everything about that memory, not just what we did but how we felt, everything we sensed, even the smells around us. I have events tucked away in my memory that I haven't wanted to talk about or think about for this very reason. I have been living my life, trying to move forward and grow through my trials and endure to the end. Isn't that enough?

Even though I don't like it, I know the answer. It's not. Some experiences require us to do more. To heal, we have to remember; to really move on, we have to forgive.

My life has taken me down a much different road than I could ever have imagined as a child. I had lots of dreams for myself. I grew up in a strong LDS family who went to church every Sunday, read the scriptures together, prayed together, and had family home evening. I faithfully served in my callings; in short, I was a "Molly Mormon." I planned to get married in the temple, to be sealed to my spouse for time and all eternity, and to put all of my energies into raising a family.

After high school graduation, I headed off to Provo to attend BYU. So far my plan was going well. But I didn't get my "Mrs. Degree" in college. I didn't even date much. "*There's still time*," I thought.

However, people I talked to had other opinions. Some told me that the prospect of my getting married after college was slim; I had missed my chance to meet my eternal companion. Well, if I wasn't going to get married anytime soon, I decided I should work hard to make a life for myself.

I got a job and quickly made friends with my coworkers, people who, while they were wonderful, weren't LDS. Over time, I found myself adopting their lifestyle instead of influencing them in a positive way with my own. More time went by and I became inactive. It was so easy to find other things to do, and I thought I was happy living in the world with my work friends.

One Saturday night, while I was living in downtown Salt Lake City and enjoying all the benefits of an urban lifestyle, my friend and I headed out for an evening on the town. We had just left my apartment when I heard my home phone ringing—cell phones were a luxury I couldn't afford. I made the decision to go back into my apartment to answer the phone. This seemingly simple choice ultimately changed the entire course of my life.

Another friend of mine, Amy,[39] was on the line. Some friends of hers were in town from New York City, her hometown, and she was headed up to Park City to meet them at a bar on Main Street. We were already going out, so we decided to join her, excited to be together.

When we got there, we were laughing and having a good time. We met her friends, three guys in town for a ski weekend. I had a few drinks, talked, and danced until the bar closed.

The guys were renting a condo in Park City, so we went over to their place. One of them started smoking marijuana. Another one, Tom, whom I had spent much of the evening talking to, continued to spend time with me. He told me he had an early flight in the morning and, since I lived downtown, asked if I could take him to the airport in the morning. I didn't think it would be a problem. My friend tried to talk me out of letting him stay with me, but I thought, *What could happen?*

I was naive and trusting.

---

39 Some names have been changed.

Tom, Amy, and I said good night to the others and headed back to Salt Lake. When Amy dropped us off at my apartment, I again told her that everything would be fine. My plan was to have Tom sleep on my sofa bed in the living room, but while I was saying good night to Amy, Tom crawled into my bed.

Great! What do I do now? I thought. I was tired and didn't want to make an issue of it; I just wanted to go to bed. I put my pajamas on and got into bed.

Tom tried to kiss me, but I pushed him away.

"Don't you want to do anything?" he asked.

"No," I said. "I just want to go to sleep." I rolled over and went to sleep.

The next morning I woke up undressed and in excruciating pain. What had happened to me? It didn't take long for me to figure it out.

Tom was lying undressed next to me.

I had experienced pain before—broken arms, a cross-country ski accident, sprained ankles, etc.—but nothing like this; it was internal and external. The pain made me want to throw up. I couldn't even stand, so I slid off the bed onto the floor. My head was spinning, and it took me a minute before I could even move. I crawled to the bathroom, which took all of my strength. I felt dirty, violated, and terrified. I turned on the shower and crawled in, then just sat in the tub as the hot water ran over me. I washed myself from head to toe, but I couldn't wash away the dirty feeling. I felt like one of those rape victims portrayed in a TV crime show. What should I do now? Call the police? I got out of the shower, dressed, and walked over to get my car, which was parked at Amy's apartment about a half a mile away. It was a cold Sunday morning in March, and while I walked, I decided what to do: I'd just take this guy to the airport and pretend nothing had happened.

So I did. I took him to the airport and met friends for brunch, all the while trying to act as if everything was okay.

Two weeks went by, and I knew something was terribly wrong with my body. I didn't feel well. I was tired all the time, and I just wasn't myself. I decided to go to the Planned Parenthood location in downtown Salt Lake City on my lunch hour, where they ran a pregnancy test. When the nurse told me I was pregnant, I broke down in tears.

"I take it this isn't a good thing," she said.

No, it really wasn't. My first instinct was to talk to my mom, so I drove to Sandy, where she was working. The moment she saw me, she knew something was wrong.

She took me back to an office, and I started to cry. I couldn't talk for what seemed like forever. Even now, thinking about this moment with my mom brings tears to my eyes. She listened attentively as I finally told her what had happened. Then, in a reassuring tone, she told me how much she and Dad loved me and that they would be there for me no matter what. I think that was the most important thing I could have heard at the time. No matter what had happened to me and what choices I had made, my parents loved me. Every child needs this kind of reassurance, especially those of us who make mistakes that break our parents' hearts.

Amy and I contacted one of her friends in New York City to see if we could get in touch with Tom to let him know I was pregnant, if nothing else. When we reached her friend Mike, he told her Tom was busy and that this was my problem. I was devastated. I think the fight went out of me right then and there. There would be no justice for me in this lifetime.

Over the years, I have come to realize that one day Tom will have to make an accounting to the Savior. He will have to look into the eyes of the Lord and explain his actions. This knowledge has brought me comfort. Facing the Lord will be harder than facing a jury; that the Lord is aware of my situation and He knows my heart is reassuring. He will be my advocate with the Father.

Our Decisions Shape Us and Our Lives

I have always had a testimony of the gospel, and experience has taught me that my Father in Heaven, like my earthly parents, loves me regardless of my choices. And at this point in my life, I needed Him more than ever. What should I do? Because I knew that whatever decision I made, I would never be the same and my life would never be the same.

Multiple people offered suggestions. One friend felt I should get an abortion because having a baby would ruin my life. That wasn't an option for me; it went against everything I believed about life down to my very core. Others suggested the obvious choice of adoption. If I did that, the baby would have a mother and a father.

These, among other thoughts, were what I turned to my Father in Heaven to ask about as I pled for His counsel and guidance. But it didn't come right away. I kept praying for answers. I couldn't make this decision on my own; too much was at stake for both me and my unborn child.

If I decided to keep the baby, it would be without the benefit of child support. Financially this would all be on me. My family would be there for emotional support and would love us both, but ultimately I would have to play both father and mother. Could I do this?

One day while I was really struggling with this decision, I called my mom from work and broke down in tears. One of my coworkers came by my desk and chided me, saying that tears were only for life and death—little did she know that I was struggling with just such a situation, but I let her remark pass because my pregnancy wasn't common knowledge at the time.

On a business trip to California, I felt impressed to purchase a *Chicken Soup for the Soul* book at the airport. While reading one of the chapters, I received an answer to my prayer. I knew I was supposed to keep the baby. A feeling of peace and comfort came over me, and my mind felt at ease for the first time in weeks. I immediately went to my hotel room and called my mom to tell her what I'd decided. She broke into tears, and my heart sank. Then, suddenly, as if someone had thrown me a lifeline, she said, "I'm so happy. I didn't know how I was going to let you give the baby up."

I started to cry, and we wept together. I was going to be a twenty-six-year-old single mom.

How would I do it?

* * *

Once I'd made the decision to keep the baby, I started making plans for the future. I had a good job. It would be hard, but we were going to be fine.

This was what I told myself so I could sleep at night.

But suddenly I didn't have time to think about the ramifications of my situation. I became so sick I could hardly take care of myself. I was deteriorating quickly, and I suppose you could say I went into survival mode. I couldn't keep food of any kind in my system and lost twenty-five pounds in nine weeks. I went to work, somehow made it through the day, and then came home to lie on the couch for the rest of the evening.

My coworkers became concerned for me. One of the ladies approached me in the copy room and asked if I had a severe medical condition. I smiled at her and told her the problem was medical, but I would be okay. I didn't think she believed me.

About a month later, two more ladies at the office pulled me aside.

Kathy looked at me with great concern and said, "I think you have leukemia. You really need to go see a specialist."

I told her I didn't have leukemia, but she didn't believe me. I tried to reassure her without divulging what was really wrong. These two women were very concerned, and they weren't going to be satisfied until they knew what was wrong, so I told them. Once their initial shock wore off, they pledged their support. I felt lucky but didn't feel better.

If this continued, I was going to end up in the hospital. The lease was up on my apartment, and I needed someone to take care of me. So my wonderful parents and my younger brother came to my apartment, packed it up, and moved me home. My mother had always been a little overprotective; she was certain I wouldn't make it through my pregnancy without her, and she was probably right.

Even though everyone seemed loving and supportive, I was depressed and felt like people were judging me. After all, I was an unwed mother. It didn't seem to matter that I was twenty-six and not sixteen. The looks some people gave me when they heard I wasn't married were heart-wrenching. I cried myself to sleep many nights as I tried to cope with the situation.

Then, one day, a colleague pulled me aside and asked me how I was doing. She looked me in the eye and said sternly, "Don't you ever hang your head down. People all make mistakes, and no one is perfect. They have no right to pass judgment on you, especially when they have no idea how you came to be in this condition." She was right, and although she wasn't LDS, you would have thought she'd read 3 Nephi 14:1–5:

> And now it came to pass that when Jesus had spoken these words he turned again to the multitude, and did open his mouth unto them again, saying: Verily, verily, I say unto you, Judge not, that ye be not judged.
>
> For with what judgment ye judge, ye shall be judged; and with what measure ye mete, it shall be measured to you again.
>
> And why beholdest thou the mote that is in thy brother's eye, but considerest not the beam that is in thine own eye?
>
> Or how wilt thou say to thy brother: Let me pull the mote out of thine eye—and behold, a beam is in thine own eye?
>
> Thou hypocrite, first cast the beam out of thine own eye; and then shalt thou see clearly to cast the mote out of thy brother's eye.

Joy and Heartache in Equal Measure

I knew fairly early in my pregnancy that I was going to have a boy and that his name was to be Joshua, so that's what we started calling him. Even people at work would ask me how Joshua was doing. Knowing that this little person was growing inside of me changed my focus, and I started thinking of the future. I now had something to put my efforts into.

One of saddest things for me at that time was that Amy stopped returning my phone calls. I never blamed her or held her responsible for what happened to me. I just wanted my friend to be a support for me, and she wasn't there. In turn, almost all the friends I had spent time with turned away as if I had contracted a highly contagious disease they were afraid of catching. I felt so alone and abandoned.

A few weeks before Joshua was born, Amy called me. She wanted to extend an olive branch. We talked, and I told her I would let her know when the baby was born, which I did. She came to the hospital to see us. And then I never saw or heard from her again.

My son was the most perfect, beautiful baby I had ever seen. Before the nurse put him in my arms, he was crying. They handed him to me, and the moment he heard my voice, he stopped.

"He knows who his mommy is," the nurse said.

I had never felt so much joy or love for another human being. I threw myself into being a mom. It wasn't easy—our first night home from the hospital we both ended up crying half the night.

As the learning curve softened, we survived. And we spent a wonderful discovery-laden first year together.

Then I went back to the doctor for my annual exam, and they ran a battery of tests, including a pap smear. Immediately after my sexual assault, they had run this same battery of tests to ensure I hadn't contracted HIV or some other STD. I had been given a clean bill of health, for which I was extremely grateful. This time, though, the doctor's office called me a few days later. The pap smear had come back abnormal, and I needed to go back in for a consultation and more tests. I sat in the doctor's office in shock as he explained that I had a cancerous strain of HPV. I'd never even heard of the disease, and not much was actually known about it at the time.

The doctor removed the cancerous cells from my cervix not long after that, and I went back every three months for a year to be checked—a regular reminder of what Tom had "given" me.

Over the next few years, I made several trips to the doctor's office. I had my cervix burned three times and had more cancerous cells cut out. It was infuriating. Not only had I gotten pregnant and was now a single mom, but I also had a disease that would affect me long into the future. Why did this have to happen to me?

I tried to let it go. I was juggling motherhood and a full-time job. I didn't have time to stew over something I couldn't change.

We lived with my parents until my son was two years old, and then we moved out on our own. Motherhood brought with it joy and heartache in equal measure. My son was a handful, but he was adorable, and I loved him so much. On the flip side, he was an abusive toddler. I often went to work with bruises. I would call my mother on my way home from work, crying because I didn't know what to do. My minor in family science, which included a parenting class, hadn't prepared me for this situation.

I remember one particular sacrament meeting when my son was hitting me in the face and I was trying to get him to calm down while trying to stay calm myself. Somehow we made it to the end of the meeting. One of the brothers in the ward walked up to me and asked me if he could speak to my son. He took my son aside and said, "You cannot hit your mother." I don't remember what else he said, but I felt better. The Lord had heard my prayers, and He was aware of my struggles and heartache. I ended up putting Joshua in karate and was able to use this activity to change his behavior. I'll always think of this as one of the tender mercies the Lord gave to me.

We Must Forgive Ourselves

In January of 2000, I was at a religious-meeting planner's convention in Milwaukee, Wisconsin, and struck up a conversation with a man not of my faith. He asked me my story, and I began to tell him some of the things that had happened to me.

He kindly interrupted and asked me, "When are you going to forgive yourself?"

Forgive myself? This idea had never occurred to me. I tried to challenge his question. He was patient with me but firm in his assertion that I needed forgiveness. I thought, *Isn't it about forgiving others? Doesn't the seventy-times-seven rule apply to my interaction with others?*

I could think of several people I needed to forgive when it came to my pregnancy, like my aunt, who had written me a well-meaning letter telling me that I needed to turn away from the path of unrighteousness and return to church, or my uncle, who told me he'd heard a little about how this child had come to be and wanted to let me know they would love him anyway.

I thought a lot about what this gentleman said. I talked to my bishop. "Do I need to forgive myself?" I asked.

His counsel was that, yes, just like we need to forgive others, we need to forgive ourselves. Not forgiving myself was holding me back.

We are often harder on ourselves than we are on others. I have learned that it is much easier to forgive someone who has wronged us than to let ourselves make mistakes and let them go. Sometimes we punish ourselves over and over again for the same mistake.

My bishop and I met several times to talk about how I blamed myself for the choices I'd made that had led to the night of my sexual assault. He suggested I read *The Miracle of Forgiveness* by President Spencer W. Kimball. I bought the book, but it sat on my shelf for a long time.

Since I didn't follow my bishop's advice, the Lord tried something else. The topic of forgiveness kept coming up in different Church meetings. That got my attention, and I went back to see my bishop.

When I walked into his office, he looked at me and said, "It's time. You need to forgive yourself and prepare to go to the temple."

We prayed together, and I asked the Lord to help me forgive myself. I felt so much peace in my heart; I walked out of the bishop's office a different person.

We Need to Forgive

Forgiveness is a process; it doesn't happen overnight. Sometimes it takes years. You may not even realize how withholding forgiveness is affecting your life. I love my son, but there were days when just looking at him made me so angry my whole body would fill with resentment. I couldn't get past how he was created. This resentment crept into our lives more frequently than I would have liked. Some days I felt completely void of all feeling toward this innocent child. I'd be lying if I said there weren't days I wished I'd given him up for adoption.

Still, I did not make the connection that I needed to forgive. You'd think I would have made the connection when each March rolled around and I would start to have panic attacks for about a week. They were really bad the first few years. I feared Tom would show up at work and take my son away. Not rational, but the fear was there just the same.

* * *

When my son was about nine years old, the time came for the birds-and-bees talk. A friend recommended a book to me, and my son and I went through it together. When we finished, he asked me if that was how he was made. I took a deep breath and told him the story. He was very quiet and very serious. I asked him if he was okay. He responded, "I'm really angry that he did that to you without your permission." He was so grown up and showed a maturity well beyond his years. He told me he needed some time to think about what I had told him. It made me angry to think that I had to have this conversation with my son. What child wants to hear that they were conceived not in love but in an act of violence?

You cannot forgive when you are angry.

Over the next year, I became progressively more ill, but not with anything Western medicine could find a reason for. The fatigue was so intense I would struggle to get through the week and then collapse on the weekend. My mom would come over and help me with Joshua on the weekends so I could sleep.

My dear Relief Society president came over to see me one day. She felt impressed to talk to me about her aunt who was an emotional-release therapist. She told me I needed to go through this therapy, that it could be the suppression of memories and emotions behind my illness.

I'd never heard of such a thing, and my realist self said, "Right . . . You've got to be kidding me." However, I couldn't stop thinking about it. I finally decided I had nothing to lose, so I called and made an appointment.

When the very skeptical me arrived at my appointment, the therapist told me all of her therapy was Christ centered and that we could only really be healed through the Atonement. Her job was to help individuals find what was hidden so they could be healed. Little did I know that I was about to have one of the most spiritual experiences of my life.

I didn't tell her anything about myself, but she told me that something had happened to me when I was around twenty-five and we needed to talk about it. I closed my eyes and started to tell her what had happened. She told me that my body was spending about 60 percent of its energy trying to repress or cope with my past and that I was ill because it could no longer manage the balance of what I was asking my body to do.

I can't explain exactly what was happening at the time, but I was focusing or meditating, and she asked me to look inward with my mind's eye. She told me I should see someone walking toward me and that I should identify who it was. To my amazement, it was a younger me, the twenty-six-year-old me. Her explanation was that when the sexual assault happened, my personality, or my psyche, split. There was the pretrauma me, who had been shut away, and the posttrauma me, who was trying to do it all. I would never be a whole person if I couldn't face what had happened to me and bring the two halves together. The funny thing was that I hadn't felt like a whole person for years and couldn't explain it until then.

She asked me to visualize hugging myself and pulling the other person back into myself. As I did so, I saw a bright light. She then told me I should see someone else. I did, and it was the Savior. He was smiling at me and beckoning me to come to Him. So I did. She asked me to picture all the negative emotion, resentment, fear, and anger and give it a physical form. It was a huge black mass. She told me to condense it down into my hands and then to hand it over to the Savior.

I looked at this black ball in my hands; it was the culmination of what seemed like a lifetime of destructive emotion. I handed it to the Lord. At that moment, I became whole again. My heart felt so light that I knew I had turned the matter over to the Lord. He was the judge. He had taken my burden.

Then she said, "He has a gift for you."

I looked, and in His hand He held an olive branch, which He handed to me. He was showing me He loved me, that I was part of His family. He hugged me, and I felt His warmth and the love He had for me throughout my whole body. I broke down and cried as though a dam had broken inside of me. I knew that it was not just the trauma but also the resentment and anger that had broken me. It had brought me to my knees physically and emotionally. The power of the Atonement became more real to me at that moment than at any other time in my life. Christ had the power to cleanse the blackness and to make me whole, to fix what was broken.

I still have no memory of the assault itself. Even now, after all these years, I don't know if that is a good thing or a bad thing. When I talked to my doctor about that night, she told me that what I was describing sounded like the effects of a date-rape drug, which had been popular at the time. Maybe if I could remember what happened to me, it would be easier to fully come to terms with the experience.

But even with not knowing all the details, I left the therapist's office that night feeling lighter than I had in years. I was finally free. I had turned my burden over to the Lord, and in the process, I had forgiven the man whose actions had caused me so much pain over the years.

In the weeks that followed, I realized that I felt like a whole person. I smiled more, I laughed more, I loved more, and I prayed more. I will forever be grateful to a Relief Society president who was in tune with the Spirit and was an answer to my prayers. I know the Lord is watching over me and that He is aware of my situation and what I need. He knows how to heal my wounds, and only He can take my burdens. He is my Savior. I know He lives and loves me. It is only through His Atonement that we can truly be made whole.

My son is now eighteen and has submitted his mission papers. We've been down a long road together. The Lord has guided me along the way and has been my partner in raising my son; I couldn't have gotten to this point without His help.

My son recently went on pioneer trek, and the leaders asked us to write a letter for our children to read while on trek. I told my son, "I may not have chosen to get pregnant, but I did choose to be your mom. I am honored to have been your mother for the last eighteen years. Even though you've grown into a fine young man, you are still my little boy, and I love you very much."

Part V
LOOKING PAST
THE PAST

9
History Has Taught Me: Forgiveness Begets Forgiveness
by Cheri Hardisty Battrick

A loaf of bread or a plate of cookies was not going to fix this. Forgiveness is hard under many circumstances. But it is particularly hard when it is needed for generational wrongs. The members of the mob who drove out the Mormons were long dead, but their prejudice lived on in their descendants—even down to the third and fourth generations, whom I now faced in Caldwell County, Missouri.

I STOOD THERE, STUNNED. ALL I had wanted to do was make a friend. I'd been trying to carry on a conversation in the produce section of the local market, and I'd thought it had been going so well. But when she'd asked my name and I'd said, "Cheri Hardisty," she'd abruptly turned and stormed away.

The blessing of having a unique name is that people remember it. In my case, my name was not linked to some horrific sin—at least not from *my* perspective. I was simply guilty of being a Latter-day Saint and of having relocated to this region. And that woman knew it. I was *the* Cheri Hardisty everyone was concerned about.

Our Realtor had explained to us, "If they find out you're Mormon, they won't sell to you." This surprised me because it was 1996, nearly 160 years since the Mormons had left the county. But we reasoned that our Realtor was a Mormon, so he would know . . .

right? As a result, when we met Mrs. Fitzgerald, the faithful Baptist woman from whom we bought our house, we dodged her question about our religion by telling her, "We attend a church in Cameron." Cameron, about thirteen miles west, had lots of different churches. We just didn't tell her *which* church. When she asked where we were from, we also answered carefully.

"I was raised in Southern California," I truthfully said while consciously omitting that we had recently moved from Salt Lake City.

When the inspiration had come to move to Missouri, frankly, I couldn't have been more surprised. In fact, I am embarrassed now to admit that I argued with the Lord about it, and I'm not in the habit of arguing with the Lord. I wasn't opposed to going to Missouri. For years, I had felt that eventually I would be in Missouri, but in my mind, it wasn't going to happen anytime soon.

"I have asked you to go," had come the heart-piercing response to my argument. The answer had taken my breath away. And when I'd reported this spiritual experience to my husband later that night, he'd wept and admitted he had known for three years that we were supposed to go. He had just been afraid to tell me.

And so it was that we were in Missouri.

* * *

As we know from modern revelation, Independence, Missouri, will one day be the center of Zion. In the Doctrine and Covenants, we read:

> Hearken, O ye elders of my church, saith the Lord your God, who have assembled yourselves together, according to my commandments, in this land, which is the land of Missouri, which is the land which I have appointed and conse-crated for the gathering of the saints.
>
> Wherefore, this is the land of promise, and the place for the city of Zion.

> And thus saith the Lord your God, if you will receive wisdom here is wisdom. Behold, the place which is now called Independence is the center place; and a spot for the temple is lying westward, upon a lot which is not far from the courthouse.[40]

"Are we going to Independence?" I asked in prayer. There was no answer. In my quest for further understanding, the Lord eventually revealed that Independence was *not* our destination. Instead, He had something more . . . *challenging* . . . in mind. We were specifically directed to establish a home in Hamilton, a small town an hour's drive northeast of Kansas City. He was sending us into the heart of Caldwell County—the same county where Far West and Hawn's Mill[41] were located, where many of the early Latter-day Saints had lived and faced persecution and from which they were ultimately driven in 1839–40 in the dead of winter.

My curiosity was piqued. Why did the Lord need me to move from Salt Lake City to Hamilton? As I pondered and prayed over this question, the answer eventually came: to soften the hearts of the people.

I found clarification for this answer in the Doctrine and Covenants: "And again, I will visit and soften their hearts, many of them for your good, that ye may find grace in their eyes, *that they may come to the light of truth, and the Gentiles to the exaltation or lifting up of Zion."*[42]

So we were going ahead of time to soften the hearts of the people toward the Church in preparation for Zion to be built sometime in the future. I had never considered that this would be needful, let alone that the Lord would need me to help prepare for the eventual

---

40 D&C 57:1–3.
41 Alexander L. Baugh, "Jacob Hawn and the Hawn's Mill Massacre: Missouri Millwright and Oregon Pioneer," *Mormon Historical Studies*, Mormon Historic Sites Foundation, Salt Lake City, vol. 11, no. 1 [Spring 2010]: 3. In this article, Baugh chronicles the research and verification indicating that Jacob Hawn of Yamhill County, Oregon, is Jacob Hawn of Caldwell County. Through this research, the proper spelling of Hawn's surname as "Hawn," rather than "Haun," is documented.
42 D&C 124:9; emphasis added.

building of Zion. I already had a love for Missouri in my heart. This mission, if you will, appealed to me.

Thereafter, as I packed in preparation to move, I imagined over and over what I would do to soften hearts when we arrived. I could see myself with a wicker basket lined in red gingham, filled with homemade cookies or a jar of jam and a loaf of piping-hot bread. And in my mind, these small gifts presented with a warm smile would be enough to cause doors to open, hugs to be exchanged, and bonds of eternal friendship to be forged.

But as I stood bewildered in the produce aisle that day, I decided that maybe I had better figure out what the residents of Hamilton had against the Mormons, because until I figured that out, no amount of homemade *anything* was going to make a difference. It wasn't just that one woman in the grocery store who had turned away from me in disgust. This kind of thing was happening to me regularly.

It had started with a visit from Mrs. Fitzgerald's minister, whose church was conveniently across the street. Her minister was more than delighted to knock on our door, welcome us to the neighborhood, and invite us to join his congregation. He was a handsome young man and pretty down-to-earth. I hadn't had much experience with other churches, so when he came in blue jeans and a plaid shirt, I was a bit surprised. But I liked him immediately, so when he invited us to come to church, I heard myself say that we would be delighted to come to a church social sometime. My husband threw me a warning look, which fortunately the minister didn't see. It was clear we had different ideas about how to soften hearts, and Brad wasn't about to attend *any* event at *any* other church.

As the minister continued in an attempt to coax us into attending Sunday services, Brad decided it was time to be absolutely clear. "We already belong to another church," he said calmly. And when the surprised minister asked which one, clearly concerned that another pastor had beaten him to our door, my husband declared, "We belong to The Church of Jesus Christ of Latter-day Saints."

The minister's eyes grew wide with anger, and his soft features hardened as his lips tightened around the words, "You're *Mormons?*" Then he turned abruptly and stomped off our porch. I couldn't help but wonder if announcing our membership in the Church had been a mistake. For the rest of the day, the tune of the lilting Primary song "The Church of Jesus Christ" ran through my head. How easy it was to sing the words that we belonged to The Church of Jesus Christ of Latter-day Saints. How easy it was for my husband to say them. But the reverberations of that one statement rippled tumultuously through the town in about fifteen minutes flat.

And from then on, we were the enemy.

* * *

Not long afterward, I found in my collection an old, worn copy of *The Missouri Persecutions.* I couldn't help but laugh because of what I was going through. I decided perhaps it would be a good idea to read it. Maybe it would help me understand why so many of my Missouri neighbors were so bitter against me.

This volume, written by B. H. Roberts, was excruciating to read. Take, for example, this passage that describes the actions of the members of the mob toward one faithful Saint:

> Thomas McBride, an old gray haired veteran of the American Revolution, was met by a number of the mob in front of Mr. Haun's house. The old man, trembling with age rather than from fear, surrendered his gun, saying: "Spare my life, I am a Revolutionary soldier." But the inhuman wretch to whom he made this simple, pathetic appeal, sufficient to have moved adamantine hearts, shot the veteran down with his own gun, and then a Mr. Rogers, of Daviess County, fell upon him and hacked him to pieces with an old corn cutter. And there lay the veteran soldier of the Revolution, covered with a score of unsightly

wounds, either of which alone had been fatal—
his brains oozing from his cracked skull, and his
white hairs crimsoned with his gore! Oh, a hard
fate to overtake one of that noble band, who gave
the best years of his life to his country's service,
that liberty might survive oppression![43]

It was gut-wrenching to read Roberts' account of the horrors
the Saints faced. Especially at Hawn's Mill and Far West, both
of which were not far from my new home. I could see the faces
of the traumatized Saints in my mind as I read. I could feel their
anxiety. And then one day, it all became quite personal for me.

* * *

When I was a young girl, my grandmother instilled in me her love for
genealogy. One day near the end of Nana's life, she summoned me
to her home and gifted me several old trunks full of her genealogical
records and family history research. There were books and old photo
albums, the kind with black pages and picture corners. There were
research notes scribbled on scraps of paper and neatly typed pedigree
charts and family group sheets.

And there was this one ancestor, Mary Jane Champlin. When I
first saw Mary Jane's name on a pedigree chart, something stirred in
my soul. It was as though she was reaching out to me from beyond
the veil, tugging at my heartstrings, asking me to notice her—to
remember her. But all I had were a few sketchy dates and places. I
went through the trunks looking for additional pieces of her life but
found none.

From then on, every time I worked on my genealogy—*every*
time I went to a family history library—I looked for her. But she was
elusive. Some ancestors are like that. That is, until shortly before we
moved from Salt Lake City to Missouri, when I became an active
member of the International Society Daughters of Utah Pioneers.
At the first camp meeting I attended in Salt Lake, I learned that
the purpose of the organization was to preserve the stories of our

43 Salt Lake City, Utah: Bookcraft, 1965, 235–6.

pioneer ancestors. And when I learned that those histories were on file at the international headquarters of the organization and that it was less than two miles from my home, I grabbed my pedigree chart and went!

I will never forget that day. The librarian and her assistant presented me with one file folder after another of histories and documents pertaining to my pioneer ancestors. Each time they brought a folder, I held my breath, hoping for something of Mary Jane. I was disappointed again and again until finally the last folder they pulled bore her name.

Tears coursed down my face as I read for the first time some of the details of her life. I sat there in the late afternoon sun at the old library table, with its warm chestnut patina, for quite some time, hardly able to breathe. At last Mary Jane was no longer just a name with a few dates. She was a real person with a *real* life. And she—my third great-grandmother—had personally known the Prophet Joseph Smith!

I purchased a photocopy of her history[44] and tenderly packed it into a box. After I arrived in Missouri, in the midst of my quest for understanding, Mary Jane's story surfaced. This time as I read it, I found clues she had left for me. Mary Jane and her family had lived in Caldwell County, Missouri. And they had survived the Hawn's Mill Massacre.

I suppose that detail had been discovered and then forgotten during my first reading of her two-page history because of how earth-shattering it had been for me to learn that she had known Joseph Smith. But now, reading it in Caldwell County, it was as though her presence was beckoning me to Hawn's Mill. So one afternoon, I set off in my car to see the place for myself. My hope was that in setting foot on the site, I would better understand the past and thus better understand my mission here in Caldwell County.

I wish I could share how green and lush the tree-lined meadow in the bend of Shoal Creek was that day. It was autumn, and the

---

44 Leah Dickson Johns, "History of Mary Jane Champlin Dickson" (unpublished manuscript from the archives of the International Society Daughters of Utah Pioneers, Salt Lake City, Utah), copy in possession of author.

leaves rustling in the wind were just beginning to turn. As I stood there, looking across the grass toward the south, I tried to imagine the small settlement, with its blacksmith shop, a few cabins, and some families living in tents and wagons. I tried to imagine the mill itself. It was a beautiful, peaceful place. I felt a special reverence for those who had lost their lives that fateful October day. And though there was no cemetery, no headstones of any kind, I knew I was standing on sacred ground.

My imaginings faded back into reality, and I realized someone had placed a wooden sign on the property. I reverently drew near this simple monument, and an unexpected chill ran up my spine. The sign was peppered with bullet holes—many of them going right through the small engraved brass plate that served as a memorial to those who had been slain. Instinctively, I whirled around, fully expecting that I had been followed there and was now in mortal danger.

But there was no one. Just a feeling that had come unexpectedly, almost like a warning. "Be careful," it seemed to say. "You could be next."

Bullet holes? I thought as I quickly drove to the safety of my home. *Really? There are still people who hate Mormons that much?*

* * *

In the months that followed, Mary Jane led me to understand what her family experienced at Hawn's Mill. It seemed as though she accompanied me often. Through the mentioning of her name, I met distant cousins who had a more thorough history of the Champlins from their ancestors. Their history fleshed out some of the details of the experience Mary Jane's family had at Hawn's Mill. She had been a child of eight years when the militia had ridden in on horseback. Her father, William Champlin, had run to the blacksmith shop, from which he intended to help defend the settlement. As bullets whizzed past, Mary Jane and her mother and sisters crossed the plank running along the top of the millpond dam and fled into the woods to hide.[45]

---

45 Delia Ann F. Allen, "To a Pioneer Mother: Angelina Avilda Champlin" (unpublished personal history from book of remembrance), copy obtained from Elizabeth

When the 1,600 rounds of ammunition the mob fired[46] were expended, the mob raided and looted the settlement. This went on for some time, but eventually the women and children dared to return. I can only imagine how relieved Mary Jane must have been when she learned that her father was still alive: "William Champlin was not only alive, but was in fact completely unharmed. Earlier, when the decision was made to abandon the blacksmith shop, he chose to remain inside rather than face what was sure to be a barrage of bullets. To protect himself from detection, he drew several of the dead bodies on top of him to make it appear as if he was one of those killed."[47]

But Mary Jane's friend Sardius Smith was dead.

> [William Reynolds], a Livingston county man, killed the little boy Sardius Smith, 10 years of age. The lad had run into the blacksmith shop and crawled under the bellows for safety. Upon entering the shop the cruel militiaman discovered the cowering, trembling little fellow, and without even demanding his surrender fired upon and killed him, and afterwards boasted of the atrocious deed to [Charles R. Ross] and others. He described, with fiendish glee, how the poor boy struggled in his dying agony, and justified his savage and inhuman conduct in killing a mere child by saying, "Nits make lice, and if he had lived he would have become a Mormon."[48]

Chipman of Cameron, Missouri (direct descendant of Angelina Avilda Champlin) in possession of Cheri Hardisty Battrick.

46 See Joseph Young, petition in Clark V. Johnson, *Mormon Redress Petitions*, as cited in Alex Baugh, *A Call to Arms: The 1838 Mormon Defense of Northern Missouri* (Provo, Utah: Joseph Fielding Smith Institute for Latter-day Saint History and BYU Studies, 2000), 123.

47 Isaac Leany, petition in Clark V. Johnson, *Mormon Redress Petitions*, 487, as summarized in Alex Baugh, *A Call to Arms: The 1838 Mormon Defense of Northern Missouri* (Provo, Utah: Joseph Fielding Smith Institute for Latter-day Saint History and BYU Studies, 2000), 123.

48 John D. Lee, *History of Caldwell and Livingston Counties, Missouri* (St. Louis: National Historic Company, 1886), 149.

The account of Sardius Smith's death traumatized me for some time. I tried to happily go about my business, but as I continually faced the jeers and taunting of those around me, many of whom I learned were descendants of that mob, I found myself fighting inside to love my neighbors. Many times, I fell to my knees and pled with the Lord for understanding. Why did he want *me* to soften the hearts of these people? At times I felt as though I was a Nephite sent to live among the Lamanites or like Jonah called to Nineveh. There were times I wanted to flee just as Jonah had.

After learning more of what my ancestors and their friends had faced, I didn't *want* to be with my neighbors, let alone reach out to them. Their ancestors had hated mine. And although not one of them knew my ancestors had been accosted by theirs at Hawn's Mill, they, nevertheless, hated me. Was it even possible to soften their hearts?

* * *

"Seek first to understand, *then* to be understood."[49] It was as though Mary Jane was whispering Stephen Covey's words to me. This counsel came to my mind more than once as I struggled to know how to move forward. And so it was that in the months that followed, I read everything I could find about Caldwell County history and the Mormon War. Before I could soften anyone else's heart, I had to find a way to soften *mine* toward them. But how?

The day I went to the Hamilton Public Library was a turning point in my understanding. It felt as though Mary Jane was leading me, coaxing me to go there to look for answers. I carefully planned my visit when it was busy so no one would notice or interrupt me. I didn't want to explain what I was looking for or why.

By then I had been banned from one of the two grocery stores in town. "We don't want Mormons in here!" the owner had announced loudly one day when I was shopping. "Don't *ever* come back!" I left without my groceries and never returned. I couldn't

---

49 Stephen R. Covey, *The Seven Habits of Highly Effective People* (New York: Free Press, A Division of Simon and Schuster, 1989), 237; emphasis added.

risk being banned from the library as well; it possibly had clues that would explain the hostility aimed at me.

I felt like a spy that day as I tried nonchalantly to find Missouri history books that Missourians had written. Although we were living in the computer age, the card catalogue was fortunately in an old wooden cabinet with drawers and drawers of carefully typed, yellowing index cards. This was the kind of card catalog I had grown up with, so I was able to peruse it without help and without worrying that someone would be able to monitor what I looked at. All the while, I prayed I wouldn't be noticed.

The bookshelves for Missouri history were in an isolated back corner of the library, almost completely encircling a distressed library table and a couple of hardwood chairs. It was there that I first read a Missouri history book written by someone with a definite bias against the Latter-day Saints. It was quite astonishing to read a version of Church history that was far different from anything I had been taught in Sunday School or seminary.

I came away from my covert research understanding that there were two completely different perspectives on the events leading up to and following the expulsion of the Mormons from the state. The Latter-day Saint perspective, with which I was familiar, was the story of a misunderstood group of religious people seeking a peaceful refuge and home. Their presence in Caldwell County, though legally granted, was unwanted. While the early Saints lived there, they were once again misunderstood. And they were finally forced from their homes with winter and the threat of death chasing them across the state.

But the story I read in the library books that day was completely different. It painted the Mormons as an odd, selfish group of religious ruffians who had come into the area and taken property, livestock, and anything else they needed *by force*. This alternative account said the Mormons had burned the homes of their Missouri neighbors and that they had started the Mormon War by committing murder in a town called Gallatin, which they then burned to the ground.[50] The Missouri histories chronicled

50 See *History of Caldwell and Livingston Counties, Missouri*, 128.

alleged hostilities the Mormons launched strongly and regularly against the hardworking Missourians who had homesteaded the land prior to the arrival of their imposing new neighbors. One history said,

> Dreadful stories were told of the conduct of the Mormons, and dreadful assertions and predictions made regarding their future if they were allowed to remain in the country. . . . Certain [Mormon] speakers had declared from time to time that "the earth is the Lord's," and that He had given certain portions of it in Missouri to His Saints, and that in time He would deliver over to them the whole world. These declarations were misquoted and distorted to the effect that the Mormons claimed all the country *then*, and regarded the Gentile settlers only as so many intruders and trespassers whom they meant to dispossess at the earliest opportunity, peaceably if they could, forcibly, if necessary. . . .
>
> It was declared that the Mormons were horse thieves and cattle rustlers and were insolent and overbearing in their demeanor.[51]

By the time I left the library that day, I was shaking. If that was what the community thought the Mormons were about, no wonder they didn't want us here. In following the counsel of our Realtor in not disclosing our religion and our origins, we had succeeded in buying property. But at what cost? By so doing, we had unknowingly perpetuated the same disturbing beliefs about Mormons these people had held and passed down for generations!

I was beginning to see that this journey would be one of forgiveness—for both sides. The question was would forgiveness even be possible? I had no idea how to make amends for what I had done. People often talk of how the words we say are like the fluff of a dandelion, blowing about, unable to be gathered up. I learned that

51 *History of Caldwell and Livingston Counties, Missouri*, 125.

what we do has the same consequences. How would I make amends with an entire county? And then how would I help them understand that all I ever wanted was to live among them in peace and be part of the community? Those were the questions I pondered and prayed about for years to come.

* * *

As I continued to be the public target of many of my neighbors, I turned inward in embarrassment. It was only natural to turn inward in the face of adversity, but it was not the best course of action. Elder David A. Bednar has explained that the Savior never turned inward, even in the darkest moments of His life. He set the example by turning outward and caring more about others than about Himself. And if we want to be like Him, we must do the same.[52] But at that time of my troubles, Elder Bednar had not yet been called to serve as an Apostle, and his book did not yet exist, so I didn't have the benefit of his counsel.

As a result, I didn't realize that in turning inward, which I did to insulate myself from the opposition, I was making things worse. I decided I wasn't ready to make any more attempts at softening the hearts of the people, so I turned toward my ward family and found solace in their companionship. Periodically I would again try to reach out to someone, always to be openly and publically rebuffed and shamed. I really was able to relate to the feelings of the early Saints who were driven from one locality to another.

And so I continued to hide.

I hid from the community by immersing myself in Church callings, Relief Society activities, and relationships with other members. It was easy to be friends with my Latter-day Saint companions. It felt safer to not reach out to those of other faiths. With the lifestyle we lead as members of the Church, which requires much, and what sometimes seems to be all of our time and talents, I felt justified.

Despite wanting to forget about the earlier prompting to soften hearts, there it was, always nagging at the back of my mind. Every

---

52 David A. Bednar, *Act in Doctrine: Spiritual Patterns for Turning from Self to the Savior* (Salt Lake City, Utah: Deseret Book, 2012), accompanying DVD.

once in a while, I would resume my study of Church history. It was during one of these times that I saw I was making the same mistake the early Saints had made in this region. History was repeating itself.

As the early Saints had gathered at Far West and other settlements throughout Caldwell County, attempting to establish a Zion community among themselves, their isolationist ways were offensive to their non-Mormon neighbors. The Saints formed close-knit communities. They traded among themselves. They were Easterners with different ways and different beliefs than the rough-and-tumble adventurous folks of Missouri. These isolationist activities served to cause more problems for them.

And what was I doing? *Exactly* the same thing. I was hiding from the community and, by so doing, was alienating myself even further. I was already viewed as a threat. But the more I retreated, the less they trusted me because *they didn't know what I was up to.* I wasn't doing anything aimed at hurting them, but because I wasn't reaching out to them, what were they supposed to think?

I didn't know what to do. I knew I needed to repent and open myself up, turn the other cheek, and love my neighbors, but now, having been largely apart from them for several years, I didn't know how to begin again.

Fortunately, the Lord did.

* * *

During the late 1990s, more members of the Church gradually trickled into Caldwell County from the western states. Each family seemed to have their own inspiring story of how they'd come to know that the Lord needed them in Missouri. It seemed as though He was sending reinforcements. God reassured me with each new move-in that I was not alone. The work of building good relationships could be accomplished.

I loved Caldwell County because rural living was so different from what I had grown up with in bustling Orange County, California. Northwest Missouri felt like stepping back in time to the 1950s. The pace of life was slow and relaxed. And as I walked or drove down the main street, I loved that every business façade had that quaint antique character. Many of the storefronts were sixty to one hundred years old and were reminiscent of movie sets from days gone by. High school football and the small community theater provided recreation and opportunities to showcase homegrown talent.

My husband drove sixty-five miles each way to work at a Kansas City bank. But the time came when gas prices increased faster than his wages, and I had to find work. We couldn't afford for both of us to commute, so I put my résumé together and began trying to network. Most of the jobs in the small eight-page community newspaper, *The Hamilton Advocate*, were for over-the-road truckers or nurses. Once in a while, a position came up for a cafeteria worker at the local school or nursing home, but none of these jobs fit my skill set. There simply wasn't a need for an executive secretary, let alone a human resources director in rural Missouri. There wasn't even a minimum-wage, fast-food job within fifteen miles.

I had another strike against me as well. In the rare cases where employers didn't know I was LDS, my résumé gave it away. Because my college experience was at Brigham Young University, it was kind of hard to hide my Mormon roots. And so it was that I ran out of job options. No one would hire me in Caldwell County or in the neighboring counties. As I fought with emotions linked to repeated rejection and the stress of *really* needing a job, I knew I had to find a way to forgive. It was as if the little song "Help Me, Dear Father," which I had learned in Primary as a child, became my mantra. It asks the Father to help each person freely forgive anyone who might seem unkind and to help us all live nearer to Him.[53]

I turned to my Heavenly Father. I pled with Him to open a door somewhere so I could find work to help support our family. I pled with Him to help me find someone who would take pity on me and, despite my religion, allow me the opportunity to work. I was ready to humble myself. I was ready to open my heart again. I was ready to change my ways and repent of hiding and reach out to others. I was ready for whatever He needed me to do.

---

53 Frances K. Taylor, "Help Me, Dear Father, " *Children's Songbook*, 99.

It was at that point that the Lord knew I was prepared enough and understood enough of the dynamics that existed to embark officially on my mission to soften hearts. I just didn't know that was what He had in mind when our financial stability was threatened.

One crisp autumn day, I was prompted to walk down the side-walk *without* my résumé to plead for work at the Harper House Tea Room. I had not approached this business before because I didn't know how to wait tables. In addition, I was Mormon, and Mormons don't drink tea. So the thought of entering a tearoom was a little intimidating. But that day, as I prayed to know where I could find work, the Spirit led me there.

Two women owned the Tea Room, and when I entered that day, I met Sylvia Anderson for the first time. Sylvia was a plump, gray-haired grandmother with a kind face and soft eyes.

"Excuse me, ma'am," I said as I approached her. "I'm looking for work. I'm *desperate* for work. I'm willing to do anything you might need, even scrubbing floors or cleaning toilets."

Her soft face softened even more. I later learned that she was the equivalent of the Relief Society president for the Baptist Church and that she was highly aware of who I was and what her minister's anti-Mormon sentiments had done to impact the community's feelings against me.

My petition did not fall on deaf ears. She wanted to help me. "Can you iron?" she asked.

Oh my goodness, could I ever. My mother was the queen of ironing and had taught me to iron from the time I was old enough to press my father's hankies.

"Do you think you could take on laundering and ironing the tablecloths for the Tea Room?" she asked.

I assured her I could.

"Well, then, you figure out how much you will charge per tablecloth, and I'll talk to my partner about it."

As we came to an agreement, it was clear to me that Sylvia was really sticking her neck out for me. Her instructions were for me to retrieve the soiled tablecloths after dark and return them in the early morning so that no one would know she had hired me. What a blessing to be employed—even if it was only at a rate of $3.50 per tablecloth. Her kindness lifted and buoyed me.

The work was hard. The exquisite white brocade tablecloths were large and antique and required starching. The colored overlay tablecloths were of a type of cloth that didn't respond well to ironing. If I didn't pull them from the dryer soon enough, the wrinkles remained, and I had to start over. And ironing was a hard task. It wasn't just the heat of the iron that made it hard. It was standing for hours and hours over an ironing board that just about killed me.

In those late-night and early-morning hours while I worked, I pondered my situation and how the Lord had truly humbled me through this experience. I thought a lot about Ammon, the Book of Mormon missionary, and how he never complained about the humble work he did. He just quietly went about tending the king's sheep and tried to be the best shepherd, the best servant, he could be. In those quiet hours of pondering, I made up my mind to follow his example. I would be the *best* tablecloth caretaker the Harper House had ever had. I wanted Sylvia and her partner, Jacque, to never regret hiring me. I wanted to show my gratitude to them through my work, for after years of my being persecuted and shunned, they were my first friends in the community.

I came to realize that the Lord called me to repentance by allowing our financial difficulties to require me to work. Through that work, He not only pulled me out of isolation, but He also opened the door for forgiveness on all sides. As time went on, Sylvia and Jacque noticed how meticulously I cared for their tablecloths. One morning while I was making my delivery to them, they asked if they could speak with me.

"We've been thinking," they said, "that you've been doing a wonderful job with the tablecloths." I thanked them for noticing. "And we've decided that we would like to promote you." My heart leaped within me as I said a silent prayer of gratitude. Promote me, they did, to bussing tables—on one condition: the only thing I was permitted to say to their customers was, "Are you finished?"

I understood without them explaining. They couldn't risk my saying something that would alert customers to the fact that I was Mormon. That would run off their business. They provided me with a darling bib-style apron to wear over my dresses, but none of us wore name tags. That was probably a good thing in order to keep my identity from being discovered. As I carefully set and cleared tables, I kept my word. The only thing I ever said to our customers was, "Are you finished?" And I made the decision to be the best busser the Harper House had ever had.

Jacque and Sylvia were wonderful to work for. They often fed me and gave me employee discounts on the Victorian gift-shop merchandise they stocked. They even sent leftovers from catering events home with me to help with my grocery budget.

One day, they came to me and again said, "We've been thinking. We want to promote you."

This time the promotion was to work side by side with them in the kitchen. I decided to be the best kitchen help the Harper House had ever had. At first I just washed and prepped the vegetables for their fresh and colorful salads. As time went on, they taught me to make their gourmet sandwiches on marbled rye bread and to plate the food beautifully for their customers. I thoroughly enjoyed working with them each day, and we became good friends.

I also made another extremely important decision. I was not ever going to talk about the Church. I felt that this decision was important and inspired. Sylvia had never asked me about my religion nor told me about hers. Neither had Jacque, who was Christian but did not affiliate with any congregation. We could have easily had meaningful conversations about religion, but I didn't feel we should. And although being a member of the Church was a big part of my life, I limited my conversation to my family, my interests, my hobbies, and my past work experience. They shared the same things about their lives with me. We bonded in our common sisterhood, and they came to understand that my intent was *not* to try to convert them to the Church.

Looking back now, I can see that they were probably quite puzzled by this because of the active missionary program of the

Church. But they never questioned me. I was determined to just let them see the impact of the gospel on my life through how I lived and how I treated them. I thought often of the scripture in the Sermon on the Mount: "Let your light so shine before men, that they may see your good works, and glorify your Father which is in heaven."[54]

One day, they came to me again. "We've been thinking," they said. "We want to promote you." This time the promotion was to wait tables and serve as a hostess at the front desk. This time there were no restrictions placed on my ability to communicate with customers. They now knew they could trust me to interact appropriately and without mentioning the Church because I had never mentioned the Church to them. As we talked, they asked if I had any Mormon friends they could hire. They liked my work ethic, and they hoped I could recommend women like me to assist them in various ways to build the business. From then on, nearly every employee they hired was a Latter-day Saint.

Two hearts had been softened. Two wonderful, generous hearts.

Then one day, Sylvia asked me to work in the kitchen with her. Something was obviously wrong.

"Cheri," she said, "I need to tell you something." As she paced back and forth, she told me that she was upset with her minister. It was then that I learned of her position in her church as a leader over the women. "Last Sunday something happened that really upset me," she said. "My pastor got up in church, and *from the pulpit*, he began criticizing the Mormons."

I held my breath, fully aware of the kinds of pulpit-pounding sermons about the Mormons that might be possible in this county.

"I couldn't take it," she said. "Right in the middle of his sermon, I just stood up. I told him in front of God and everyone that he didn't know what he was talking about. I told him that I had hired Mormons—plenty of them—and that I had found them to be kind and loving and God-fearing people. I told him that I would not stay and listen to any more talk of the Mormons. I told him if he or anyone else wanted to meet a Mormon to find out for themselves,

54 Matthew 5:16.

all they had to do was come to the Tea Room. And then . . . I stormed out!"

I just about fell over.

Inside, my heart was rejoicing at the thought that she had come to love us so much that she would make a public statement in our defense, especially in that setting and to that minister— the one who had stormed off my porch. Her position as a leader over the women would surely cause those in her care to consider her testimony of the Mormons. Things were definitely looking up.

Not long after that, Jacque and Sylvia came to me. "We've been thinking," they said. "We'd like to promote you." This time the promotion was to serve in a newly created position of marketing representative.

I told them I didn't have any experience with marketing.

They told me it was okay. I had the experience they needed.

I was puzzled until they explained that they had decided they wanted to open the Tea Room to the LDS tour buses that passed through the community every day on their way between Far West and Nauvoo. "We've been checking," they said. "Those buses have to travel clear to Jamesport for a meal. We could provide lunches right here—right in Hamilton—and give them the opportunity to see that Caldwell County can be friendly to the Mormons."

I accepted this final promotion immediately.

Business at the Tea Room increased exponentially. On days when the bus tours came for lunch, we seated them in the restaurant, on the porch, on the front lawn under the large hundred-year-old trees, and in the gazebo. We set the tables with beautiful linens and Victorian centerpieces. We wanted our LDS guests to know they were welcome here. The entire community saw that busses were coming to the Tea Room and began to realize that having the Mormons in town could bless their businesses too.

Then one day it happened.

It was a typical Monday, and the Monday Club was coming to the Tea Room for their monthly luncheon. The Monday Club was a group of astute and highly influential women in Hamilton. They were the movers and shakers. Their husbands held positions of trust and power in the community, and that particular day, I donned an apron and was working as both hostess and waitress to them. As I waited on the Monday Club, I couldn't help but overhear their conversation.

"I don't know what to do," one of the women said. "She just up and quit!"

A hush fell over the group.

"I have no idea where we're going to find another director for the Christmas show."

As they continued talking, I learned that the Christmas show funded the heating bills for the theater during the hard Missouri winters. Without that show, there wouldn't be funds to pay for heating, and the pipes would freeze. And if the pipes froze, the potential for damage to the theater was great.

As I said before, the community wholeheartedly supported the periodic productions at the Hamilton theater.

I could not only hear the distress in their voices, but I could *feel* it too. As I retreated to the front desk to help another group of customers, the oddest feeling came over me. I felt like I was supposed to help the Monday Club. But how? As they continued eating and talking, the impressions continued. *You need to offer to direct the Christmas show.* When I heard these words in my heart and mind, I thought, *No way. I can't direct a Christmas show! The only experience I have with directing is doing one fifteen-minute roadshow.* I was not skilled enough to direct a production at a community theater.

But the Lord felt differently.

Over and over, the impression came that I needed to volunteer until finally I couldn't take it any longer. As the women from the Monday Club came to the front desk to pay for their lunches, I mustered my courage and spoke to the woman who seemed to be their leader. "I couldn't help overhearing what is happening with the Christmas show for the theater," I said, trying to be casual despite my wildly pounding heart.

Before I could say another word, she blurted out excitedly, "Are you a *director?*"

I smiled and managed to say, "I've done a *little* directing," and I held up my thumb and index finger with their tips very close together to show her how little.

"Then you *must* come to our theater board meeting tonight!" She wrote down a few details for me and asked me to bring my ideas so we could get started. The show was to be in less than three weeks.

* * *

There are times when the Lord asks us to do hard things. And there are times when the Lord seems to ask the impossible. I knew the Lord was in charge and that although I was feeling this was impossible, I trusted He knew what He was asking of me. Acting in faith, I moved forward.

At the meeting that night, I was officially named the director of the Christmas program. It was to be a Christmas variety show, with singing and dancing, acting, and even a live nativity. We named it "Winterfest," and everyone was sure I could pull it off beautifully.

I felt a tad overwhelmed. I didn't know anyone to put in the show from the community except for a couple of people whose names the theater board had given me and Susie Millet, a friend of Sylvia and Jacque. The only other resources I had were members of the Church. And with just three weeks to prepare, all I could do was go to them and ask for their help.

The show went well. And unbeknownst to the audience, Mormons were everywhere! They were singing and dancing and having a wonderful time. The ward choir sang several Christmas pieces, and the youth performed a winter waltz from their roadshow that past summer. A sister from one of the neighboring branches who had a dance studio brought her students to perform several numbers. Those who played instruments played. Those who sang in small groups sang. And the live nativity was performed to music by—you guessed it—the Primary children.

We played to a sell-out crowd that night. Only in a small town would people pay good money for such a homespun show. And they absolutely *loved* it.

At the theater board meeting the week after the show, the board members were buzzing with excitement. "We made enough to pay the winter heating bills!" they announced when I arrived, and a spontaneous cheer went up.

As we congratulated and hugged each another, one of the women paused and said, "Cheri, that was a *wonderful* show. Where did you find all those talented people?"

My heart stopped. I took a deep breath and said as casually as I could, "Oh, they are members of my church."

"What church do you belong to?" she innocently asked. It was the moment of truth, and my mind flashed back to the day the minister had asked that very same question of my husband and me as he'd stood on our front porch.

I paused and then said with as much joy in my voice as I could muster, "I belong to The Church of Jesus Christ of Latter-day Saints."

"You're a *Mormon*?" they all said, almost in unison.

And then one of them asked in a hushed and reverent tone, "The Mormons . . . came to help us in our time of need?"

I smiled, not knowing what to say. Yes, the Mormons, who all along had wanted nothing more than to be a part of the community, had come to their aid. Quietly and unassumingly, without announcing themselves and without asking anything in return. As this realization dawned on the committee, their faces softened, their eyes glistened with tears, and the Spirit softened their hearts. Every last one of them. And a spirit of forgiveness descended upon that room and upon those women.

Word of the service the Mormons had rendered spread throughout the community almost faster than the word that the Mormons had moved into town had. In the months and years to come, the Lord worked a miracle in Hamilton and in Caldwell County. It started that night at the theater, and it grew and grew. Mormons were needed and asked to serve in many ways. We were invited to permanently join the theater board, to be in charge of the annual Christmas tree lighting event, and to serve on the board of directors for the newly formed Caldwell County Business Association.

Eventually, on September 22, 2002, the Church created a Hamilton Branch—the first branch created in Caldwell County since the Saints had been driven out. In the wake of this miracle, the branch was often called upon to participate in community events. We were asked to provide family history research training at the American Legion building during the annual Gas and Steam Engine Show each year. We were invited to take the lead in hosting the annual Christmas Day dinner for the hundreds who had no place to go and to deliver Christmas dinner, with the help of the other churches in the community, to hundreds of homebound and elderly residents. We formed a sixty-voice interdenominational choir, with Jacque and me as coconductors, and practiced at the LDS chapel in Cameron. People of all faiths attended. We even hosted an annual community Fourth of July pancake breakfast at the Far West Temple site.

As I was trying to do my part in softening hearts, and as the branch did theirs, the Lord had been quietly working through others in the community as well. My friend Shelia encouraged Anne Tezon, the beloved local owner and editor of the newspaper, to visit Salt Lake City so she could learn about the Church firsthand. This trip changed Anne's perspective about the Mormons, and she returned to Caldwell County determined to use the power of the pen through her newspaper to help others change their perspectives too.

Recently Anne shared with me what prompted this decision:

> As I recall it, we were traveling back to Missouri following a wonderful trip to Salt Lake City, with tours of Welfare Square and seats at a performance of the Mormon Tabernacle Choir, when a powerful inspiration struck me. The way that I could help erase the bogeyman shadow from LDS members would be to start a series of stories

about all the churches in the county. I would attend services, interview pastors, list or outline
doctrines and essentially be a public relations
agent for the churches, all of whom were facing dwindling memberships. Naturally, the LDS
story would not be first or last. But I would be
able to list the church principles and give people
a glimpse of how dedicated and loving the Latter-
day Saints can be and how dedicated they are to
serving their local communities.[55]

Anne's resulting column, "The Ecumenist," changed hearts,
fostered tolerance, and built incredible unity. It not only helped the
community understand the doctrines and culture of the Mormons,
but it also helped build bridges and soften hearts in *all* of the
churches and *all* of the community members toward one another.

* * *

In the ensuing years, my life changed drastically when my husband
and I divorced and I needed to find a roommate.

Lora Prewitt filled that role. When we first met, she made it
clear there were two things that we would never discuss: religion or
politics. She belonged to the Shelburne Baptist Church in Grundy
County, of which her family and extended family had been members forever. She introduced me to her family, who were warm and
wonderful people. We spent holidays and birthdays together. I even
sampled hog brains on one occasion, which weren't half bad. Having the Prewitt family in my life was instructive and healing. They
taught me more about how to fit in and more about how to be
inclusive than I think anyone else could have.

Several years later, I married again in the Nauvoo Temple, and
life changed even more. Lora came with us to Nauvoo and waited
outside the temple with the grandchildren I was inheriting. Sylvia
catered the wedding luncheon, and the whole Prewitt family came
to wish us well at the reception. It was a lovely celebration.

---

55 Anne Lorene Tezon; private e-mail to Cheri Battrick, October 3, 2015.

At the time I remarried, my desire was to stay in Hamilton. Not only was it my home, but the community members were also my *friends*. I wanted my new husband, Craig, to know them—to love them—like I did. But in the end, I left my house in Lora's care and moved to Craig's farm near Adam-ondi-Ahman. While we were living on the farm, the Church created the Far West Ward, which took in the town of Hamilton. The community was ready for it. The members of the Church were ready. Hearts had been softened and relationships repaired.

Although I had moved to the farm, shortly after the creation of the ward, the president of the Caldwell County Area Business Association asked for my help. They wanted a display to tell the story of the early Mormon settlers' journey . . . as it related to Hawn's Mill! I was asked to work with a prominent woman whose ancestors had lived in the county at that time, and we were charged with telling the story from both points of view to show the journey the two of us had taken in finding forgiveness and becoming friends. That was when I knew that forgiveness and healing were complete. I felt like a missionary whose investigators had just set a baptismal date!

However, it was not to be. At this incredibly climactic time, the Lord decided to transfer my husband and me to Utah. I could hardly believe it. My mission in Caldwell County had come to an end. As we held the garage sale of the century at the Hamilton house in preparation to move, the community turned out in droves, with many of them returning multiple times during the three-day stretch. We asked them to take what they needed and pay only what they could. Most came with pennies and nickels, all they could find or spare as the unemployment rate was staggering. My friends went away with what they needed, leaving behind items they knew their neighbors needed. It was truly consecration for all of us.

But the best part was the love we all felt for one another. It was extraordinary. I didn't want to leave them, and they didn't want me to go. Their repeated requests begging me to stay in Missouri bonded my heart to theirs forever. It seemed as if we had fulfilled the scripture that says, "And the Lord called his people Zion, because they were of one heart and one mind, and dwelt in righteousness; and there was no poor among them."[56]

Mary Jane Champlin's influence and guidance from beyond the veil taught me that I needed to repent and not judge. The Lord allowed financial difficulties to open the door so I could serve the community with my whole heart. Service taught me to love. Love softened my heart and allowed me to forgive. And forgiveness begat . . . forgiveness.

On October 18, 2015, the Far West Stake was created. It was the first stake to be created within the boundaries of Caldwell County since the Mormons were driven out in 1839.

---

56 Moses 7:18.

10
Palestinian Perspectives: Forgiving My Israeli Enemies

By Sahar Qumsiyeh

"*ROKH 'AL BEIT!*" THE ISRAELI soldier screamed at me angrily. "You can't enter Jerusalem! Go back!"

I paused, disappointed because being turned away meant I would have to find a different way to enter Jerusalem in order to go to the LDS Church services at the BYU Jerusalem Center. It meant that I would be late for church because going on the back road would take two additional hours, at least, if I could even get through that way.

It was a clear spring day in 1997. Just a few minutes before, I'd left my home in Beit Sahour. Just like any normal Sabbath, I had argued with my mom, who did not want me to go to church. I also knew that when I returned from church that day, I would get the silent treatment from both of my parents for two days. But I was looking forward to being among members of the Church, those who shared my beliefs.

It had been a year since I'd joined The Church of Jesus Christ of Latter-day Saints, and being the only LDS woman in Bethlehem often made me feel lonely. My family did not support this new faith I'd embraced and actually ridiculed it every chance they got. This was why I never told them how difficult it was for me to get to church, nor about the dangerous situations I had been in.

I had climbed hills and walls and hidden from Israeli soldiers as I'd sneaked into Jerusalem each Sabbath to go to church. I'd been shot at, attacked, and almost arrested. But none of that had swayed me. I needed the spiritual nourishment that came from partaking of the sacrament and being with my fellow members in the Jerusalem Branch.

I was born in Jerusalem, so this soldier's forbidding me to enter the city seemed unjust and cruel. Palestinians like me, who lived in the West Bank, were not allowed to enter Jerusalem, and restrictions on our movement increased every year.

I tried to form a sentence to protest the soldier's harsh demand, despite the fact that I knew he did not speak Arabic, to convince him that I needed to get through. I stared at his face and at his brown uniform and at the M-16 rifle that hung on his shoulder. The sound of those rifles was still vivid in my memory, having seen them injure and kill my people and break the bones of Palestinian youth many times.

The soldier's expression was cold as he looked at me with disgust. I thought about what to say as my own feelings of hate, anger, and impatience rushed to the surface.

It was then that I heard a still, small voice whisper in my ear. The voice was so clear, and it penetrated deep down into my heart; I heard the words of the Savior: "Ye have heard that it hath been said, Thou shalt love thy neighbour, and hate thine enemy. But I say unto you, Love your enemies, bless them that curse you, do good to them that hate you, and pray for them which despitefully use you, and persecute you; That ye may be the children of your Father which is in heaven."[57]

With the words *Love your enemies* still ringing in my ears, I looked at the soldier. *Love my enemies?*

The Lord's voice was clearly directed at me.

My initial thought was, *How can the Lord expect me to forgive and love these soldiers? Is that even possible? After what I have seen some of them do, He cannot possibly expect me to forgive and even love them!*

---

57 Matthew 5:43–44.

* * *

My hate for Israeli soldiers started when I was a teenager and steadily increased over the years. As a child, I'd feared them. When I was in elementary school, the older girls had demonstrated against the occupation. We, the younger students, had stayed inside the classroom. The Israeli soldiers came and threw tear gas toward the school, and even though we kept our classroom door and windows closed and stayed inside, we still smelled it. Our throats and noses burned, and we didn't have onions or anything else to make the effect any easier to bear.

As we heard the commotion outside and the sound of the bullets, we shivered in fear, hoping it would be over soon. I can still picture the fear on my friends' faces in the fifth grade when a student opened our classroom door and a tear-gas bomb rolled inside. Nothing the teachers did could calm us down. We wanted to go home—but it wasn't safe for us to leave. Hungry, confused, and frozen with fear, we could do nothing but wait.

When the teachers finally announced that we could go home, however, I was not relieved. I knew we had to pass the Israeli soldiers in the street in order to get to our homes. My young mind imagined the soldiers shooting me. As I passed by them, walking as closely as I could to my schoolmates, my heart beat so fast and so loud I thought the soldiers could hear it and sense my fear.

As a teenager, I became more aware of the demonstrations and the reason people organized them—these soldiers had taken away our land, freedom, and identity. And each time my Palestinian flag rose high in the air, I felt short-lived joy at the sight of it. Then part of me died each time as the Israeli soldiers would force a Palestinian, at gunpoint, to take the flag down and burn it.

In stifling heat or steady rain, I often stood in long lines with other Palestinians trying to get permission from the Israeli government officials stationed in Bethlehem to leave the country. Even after hours of waiting, we would often have to go home at the end of the day and come back to try again. We, the Palestinians, were more often than not denied the right to travel.

I experienced this when my sister, Samar, who lived in Jordan, had her first baby and I was going there to help her. The Israeli commanding officer said I was denied the exit permit because I was a troublemaker. That was preposterous. I was a seventeen-year-old girl who was uninformed of the political turmoil and complexities around me. What trouble was I making?

When I was finally granted permission to leave the country a few months later, I learned what my people experienced each time they crossed the bridge between Israel and Jordan. Israeli soldiers emptied our bags on the counter and searched every item, even our underwear. And body searches were the worst. I knew about it and dreaded having to go through it. I tried to let my brain wander to distract myself from what was about to happen. I dragged my feet toward the large pile of shoes on the bridge and placed mine there, then proceeded to the booth, doubly concerned because I had my period. I knew I had to remove all my clothes, and I was very shy about my body. I did not want to take off my underwear. I walked into the booth, and a young female Israeli soldier entered. In broken Arabic, she demanded that I take everything off. I slowly proceeded to take off my pants, my shirt, my undershirt . . . I stopped with only my underwear on, staring at the soldier. My eyes were silently begging, *Please don't make me take this off.* For some reason, she was merciful to me. After she searched my nearly naked body, I sighed in relief when she demanded that I put my clothes on again.

* * *

As these memories flooded my mind, there was one image engraved in my mind that would not leave. It was the image of the lifeless body of my fellow student Isaac. It was that particular incident, almost ten years earlier, that made my heart unable to forgive those soldiers.

The day was October 29, 1987. After a demonstration the students at Bethlehem University had organized, the soldiers surrounded the campus and would not let any of us leave. We had to stay inside the university buildings as the tear gas filled the grounds outside. We were in the science department, as far away as possible, but we could still smell it. A few injured students were being brought into our small science-department clinic, some unconscious from the tear gas and some from bullet wounds. That small clinic was not equipped to handle any form of serious injury; however, they were forced to do their best, as the soldiers did not allow anyone to leave the university. Blood now splattered the hallway floors, the same hallways that had been filled with students hurrying to their classes only hours before.

Suddenly a student named Isaac was carried in. Thick silence blanketed the crowded hallways because everyone knew this injury was different from the others. Isaac had been on the roof of the cafeteria hanging a Palestinian flag when an Israeli soldier had shot him in the head. We had expected Isaac to be rushed to a hospital, but he had not. The soldiers had not allowed it. All the students stood silently. There was nothing we could do. Nothing else mattered as Isaac slowly died.

The mayor of Bethlehem spoke to the soldiers, and they finally allowed Isaac to be taken to a hospital in Bethlehem. The doctor rolled him away as we all lined up on each side. He looked as if he was asleep, even smiling on one side of his face, but he looked dead from the other side where the bullet wound was visible. After Isaac was gone, the students started singing patriotic songs. I felt power and consolation in one of the songs: "It is all right if we die if we will root out death from our land."

What happened at the university that day changed my life forever. Isaac, who was the oldest child in his family, was a senior majoring in English literature. His parents were unable to find work and were anxiously awaiting Isaac's graduation so he could work to support the family. When soldiers took Isaac away from the hospital in Bethlehem only a short time after he was admitted, we did not know whether he was dead or alive. We later learned that his body was taken to an Israeli hospital, where many of his organs were transplanted into Israeli patients. At midnight, soldiers brought Isaac's body to his home in the Aida refugee camp and allowed only the parents to accompany the transport of their son's body to a remote field far from Bethlehem. The soldiers dug a hole and threw Isaac's body in, then covered the hole with rocks and dirt. I can't imagine how Isaac's parents must have felt that night as they saw their beloved son's body being desecrated like that.

Following the events of that day, by Israeli military order, Bethlehem University was closed and remained closed for two years. For a long time afterward, I sat in my room contemplating what had happened. I tried to understand why the soldiers would do something so inhuman. I allowed hate and anger to linger in my heart.

It might be possible for me to overcome the humiliation, loss of identity, and injustices enacted upon me and my people, but there was no way I could ever forgive or forget the act of cruelty committed against Isaac. I could not erase that image or the events of that day.

Now, almost ten years later, though, I was standing at the checkpoint, looking into the eyes of one of those soldiers, and Heavenly Father was telling me to love and forgive him. This meant I had to forgive the very soldiers who had unjustly killed Isaac and desecrated his body.

How could Heavenly Father expect this of me? Surely He could see that this was simply not possible, considering all the pain the soldiers had caused me and my people. Too shocked by what I had just been commanded to do, getting to church became secondary to me. How could I even partake of the sacrament, seeing that I was unable to obey a direct command from my Lord to love my enemies?

With a heavy heart, I turned around to go home. I walked through the fenced pathway that led out of the checkpoint. I looked back at the soldiers and saw that they were turning many people back and denying them entry to Jerusalem. Women were arguing with the soldiers, some telling them they had to go to the hospital, showing them medical records, some saying they must go to work or school, but the soldier in charge, again with a rude voice, told them what he had told me a few moments earlier: "Go home."

Love your enemies. At that moment, it became clear to me that this was a commandment from my Savior, just like any other commandment. He was asking me to love and forgive the Israeli soldiers.

Why would the Savior give me a commandment that was impossible to obey? I thought, especially when I was preparing to go to the temple for the first time. Failing to obey this commandment would render me unworthy to enter the Lord's house.

I knew in my heart that when He gave me a commandment, He also provided a way for me to obey it.[58] But even though I knew that principle to be true, every attempt on my part to love and forgive those soldiers was in vain. My hard heart simply could not do it! I prayed for guidance and help but could not feel any change.

After days of spiritual turmoil and confusion, I was reading my scriptures when I came across these words: "Wherefore, my beloved brethren, pray unto the Father with all the energy of heart, that ye may be filled with this love, which he hath bestowed upon all who are true followers of his Son, Jesus Christ; that ye may become the sons of God; that when he shall appear we shall be like him, for we shall see him as he is; that we may have this hope; that we may be purified even as he is pure. Amen."[59] I felt like the prophet Mormon was speaking directly to me. His words penetrated deep into my heart. I pondered them over and over. Mormon was telling me that if I desired with all my heart to have charity, I could pray to Heavenly Father and He could help me obtain it.

Can the Savior really teach me how to forgive and love? I knew I could not find love for those soldiers, nor could I forgive them by my own power alone. My mortal heart simply could not let go of the past. I needed the Atonement. I needed the Savior's enabling

---

58 See 1 Nephi 3:7.
59 Moroni 7:48.

power and His perfect love to fill my heart. His last words as He hung on the cross in agony were, "Father, forgive them; for they know not what they do."[60] As an astonishing example to me, the Savior was able to forgive the soldiers who crucified Him. He did not only forgive them, but He also prayed for them. The soldiers I was trying to forgive certainly hadn't whipped me or crucified me, so how could I justify not forgiving them? The words of Mormon helped me realize that charity is a gift from God. Heavenly Father is the source of all love. Just like He can plant a seed of faith in our hearts, He can also plant a seed of love.[61] Even when we can only desire to have faith, the Lord gives us the seed to nourish. I realized that the same principle applied with charity. When our hearts are unable to forgive and love, even a little, there is help from above. We simply must desire with all our hearts to have charity and then ask for His help.

I determined to do just that. So almost a week after that incident at the checkpoint, I went to my room and closed the door. I knelt and prayed with all the energy of my heart. I asked Him to show me how to love and forgive. I told Him that my human heart was hard and unable to do this without His help.

I must say I was disappointed because I had expected a miraculous change in my heart and my feelings right away. That did not happen. But I continued to fast and pray, confident that one day my prayers would be answered.

* * *

It happened on a nice Sabbath day almost a year later as I tried to cross that same checkpoint. The soldier, with his angry voice, yelled, "Go home. You are not allowed through."

I looked up at the soldier and started to protest and beg him to let me go to church. It was the same setting as the year before, with what could have been the very same soldier at the post, although most likely not. At that same place a year earlier, I'd heard the Savior's inviting commandment to love my enemies. This time

---

60 Luke 23:34.
61 See Alma 32.

everything seemed to be the same, except for one thing—my heart. This time as I looked into the soldier's eyes, my heart was filled with love instead of hate. My feelings of complete forgiveness and love actually shocked me. I had been unaware of the gradual change in my feelings and had still been questioning my ability to love. But as I looked at that solider that day, I saw a brother—a brother, not only because Palestinians and Israelis were related by blood but because in front of me stood a son of God, beloved of Him. I could feel Heavenly Father's love for that soldier.

It seemed as if I could isolate every bad thing I had seen the soldiers do from the people themselves. I still hated those acts, but my hate for the people themselves was gone. I was finally able to love my enemies! This feeling of charity and forgiveness did not come from me. God had given me these feelings because of my faith in the Atonement of Jesus Christ, because I'd had faith in Him and asked for His help. It was the Savior who had filled my heart with His love.

From this experience, I learned that with the Savior's help, I can love and forgive others, even those who have hurt me and my loved ones. I can do this because the Savior is my example. He is the only one who suffers long, envies not, and thinks no evil.[62]

Corrie ten Boom, a Dutch Christian woman, was an example to me about learning to forgive. She suffered in a concentration camp with her sister, Betsie, who died at the camp. One day, years later, after she had given a talk about her experiences and spoken on the topic of forgiveness, one of the guards at the Nazi camp she'd been confined in approached her. These are Corrie's words about the experience:

> "'How grateful I am for your message, *Fraulein*,' he said. 'To think that, as you say, He has washed my sins away!'"
>
> "His hand was thrust out to shake mine," Corrie recalled. "And I, who had preached so often . . . the need to forgive, kept my hand at my side.

---

62 See 1 Corinthians 13.

"Even as the angry, vengeful thoughts boiled through me, I saw the sin of them. . . . Lord Jesus, I prayed, forgive me and help me to forgive him.

"I tried to smile, [and] I struggled to raise my hand. I could not. I felt nothing, not the slightest spark of warmth or charity. And so again I breathed a silent prayer. Jesus, I cannot forgive him. Give me Your forgiveness.

"As I took his hand the most incredible thing happened. From my shoulder along my arm and through my hand a current seemed to pass from me to him, while into my heart sprang a love for this stranger that almost overwhelmed me.

"And so I discovered that it is not on our forgiveness any more than on our goodness that the world's healing hinges, but on His. When He tells us to love our enemies, He gives, along with the command, the love itself."[63]

For years I allowed anger and hate to destroy me. As Mormon so clearly testifies, I also testify to you that charity toward others and forgiving them is essential for our spiritual well-being—essential not only because it is a commandment from God but also because letting go of anger and hate is liberating.

One day as I was crossing a checkpoint, my friend and I waited in line for a long time. We waited for an hour, and when it was almost our turn, the soldier at the gate said, "This path is closed. Go to a different line."

After this happened two or three times, my friend got upset and yelled at the soldier.

Later she asked, "How can you deal with this injustice and not get angry?"

I told her that if I let myself get angry each time something like this happened, I would be angry all my life. As I learned to love my enemies, I also realized that at some point in my life, I had

63 In Timothy J. Dyches, "Wilt Though Be Made Whole?" *Ensign*, November 2013.

to learn to let go. Being angry and hateful toward others only hurt me. My faith and feelings of peace have intensified by learning to love and forgive, as our Savior, Jesus Christ, exemplified.

One day during our Relief Society lesson, the teacher taught us about forgiveness. She told us that the Savior was able to forgive everyone who ever harmed Him. She then asked us to think of someone in Christ's life, especially someone who had done something that seemed unforgivable.

Comments came from around the room, and after a few suggestions—Pilate, the crucifiers, etc.—everyone agreed that it was Judas, who had betrayed Christ. Jesus chose Judas as one of His Apostles; He taught Him and loved Him. Then Judas went out and betrayed Christ without a second thought.

The teacher then asked, "Do you think the Savior will forgive Judas for what he did?"

There was silence across the room. None of the sisters knew what to say. It was in that moment of silence that I pondered this question. As I thought about it, my eyes met the eyes of the Savior in a picture that hung at the front of the room. I looked at that picture, still pondering the question. All of a sudden, I heard a voice whisper, "I already have forgiven him."

I testify that the Savior can heal and soften our hearts so that we are able to forgive and love as He does. When we let go of our anger, we allow Christ into our lives, and He brings us peace and joy. He fills our lives with love.

Letter to the Reader

THE RESPONSE TO *I Can Do Hard Things with God* was overwhelming. I heard from thousands of readers who were inspired to do their own hard things. Reading letters and talking to men and women all over the world, I heard about the connections they felt to the stories and, thus, to God. The power of telling true, honest stories is what has compelled me to compile *I Can Forgive with God*.

The hearts of men are in danger of growing cold. Hurt, if allowed to linger too long, extinguishes hope and healing. These stories of forgiveness have overwhelmed me with emotion. I have cried and rejoiced as each woman has told her own personal story of forgiveness. In the world today, we need more talk of forgiveness because "all things shall be in commotion; and surely, men's hearts shall fail them, for fear shall come upon all people."[64]

My hope for this book has been that it will lead to healing and forgiveness. I pray that it too will be shared, read, and given as *I Can Do Hard Things with God* was to those who were hurting. The most courageous work done is the work of the heart. Forgiveness is an inside job. That work can't be observed, and we don't see the struggle that accompanies this private path.

I invite you to start your own journey of letting go of resentments and receiving forgiveness for your own imperfections so that

---

64 D&C 88:89–91.

fear can be extinguished and your heart can heal with forgiveness—with God. I also invite you to visit the companion website at www.icanwithgod.com, where you can get to know the women in this book and maybe share your own personal story of healing and forgiveness.

With love, Ganel-Lyn Condie

About the Author

GANEL-LYN KNOWS ANYTHING IS POSSIBLE with God. She never dreamed of writing when she graduated from Arizona State University with a BS in elementary education and psychology, yet she has become an award-winning journalist and was editor of *Wasatch Woman* magazine. She has interviewed well-known public figures, including Cokie Roberts and Richard Paul Evans, and has a talent for sharing other people's stories. She loves being a wife and mother and will always be grateful for her family. They and her faith helped her heal from a chronic illness and years of chemotherapy treatments. They've truly been instruments in the Lord's hands in many other ways. Because of her experiences, Ganel-Lyn has a passion for creating balance, organization, and spirituality in life and at home. She has discovered the joy of sharing experiences with others through her newspaper column, consulting, public speaking, and her website, www.ganellyn.com.